ALTON

Altonah
© 2016 by Ron Stone
All works of art reproduced in this book are copyrighted by Robert Duncan and may not be copied or reproduced without the artist's permission. For information regarding Robert Duncan art prints, collectibles and other products please contact:

Robert Duncan
www. robertduncan.com
All rights reserved. No portion of this book may be reproduced in any form without the written permission of the Publisher.

Design and production by:
Robyn's Hood & Associates
P.O. Box 16
Midway, Utah 84049
96 97 dlivoe 8349 898 89210238 6

Keri McWhirter, Graphic Designer

Every Child

deserves an Altonah.

This was mine.

Chapters

Chapter 1. 1

Chapter 2 13

Chapter 3 26

Chapter 4 40

Chapter 5 53

Chapter 6 71

Chapter 7 79

Chapter 8 83

Chapter 1

I was six years old riding in the back window ledge of an old black Chevrolet coupe.

My placement didn't seem like a sacrifice. It was a lot easier than being crammed between Mom and Dad and taking Dad's elbow to the pit of my stomach every time he stuck the on-the-floor gear shift into first or fourth. Mother's lap had ceased being an option since my little brother had been born.

I began having second thoughts about my window perch, however, as Dad turned off the graveled road into the rutted lane that led to the ranch. I bounced wildly against the glass as Father gunned the car trying to avoid letting the muddy claws of the road grab hold of the tires. Within moments though, I could tell we were in trouble. The tires sent out a loud scream. The car rocked back and forth and then died. I looked at the back of Dad's head. His ears came up. I knew from experience he was clenching his teeth. He didn't say anything.

Mom broke the silence. "Daddy should be coming with the team. He would have known the road was too muddy for the car."

It wasn't a minute before Daddy Clarence appeared over the horizon driving a team of horses.

I had called him "Daddy Clarence" since I learned to speak. He was my grandfather, but in my early years I had begun calling him "Daddy" while my Father was away working on the forest. That was a job he took in the summers after his employment as a schoolteacher concluded. To keep everything straight, I had been taught to add "Clarence" on to the "Daddy". I'm not sure that makes sense even now, but evidently it worked for the adults at the time…and it stuck.

I climbed out of the car and stood as tall as I could on the running board. I waved at the large figure driving the team toward us. Daddy Clarence waved back. I was really happy to see him. He had never seemed like an adult person to me. He was always just a very big friend. This year my Mother, baby brother, and I were coming to spend the entire summer while Dad worked on the forest.

Daddy Clarence spoke to me first as I suspected he would. "Ronnie, let's you and me hitch up Maude and Jane to this bucket of bolts." He turned the team and backed them up to the Chevrolet. He handed me the reins. I felt very important with Mom and Dad sitting helplessly in the car while I helped rescue them.

Daddy Clarence got down on one knee. He sank into the mud as he hooked a logging chain to the car's bumper. He got up and took the reins from my hands and draped them around his neck. He lifted me and swung me onto the back of old Jane. She was a wide horse. I grabbed the two brass balls that stuck up from the harness collar she wore.

Daddy Clarence then clucked his tongue and the two horses dug in their back feet and pulled. The Chevrolet lunged forward, and we were moving. Daddy Clarence whispered to me so Mom and Dad wouldn't hear. "This is the way man was meant to travel." I gathered he was right.

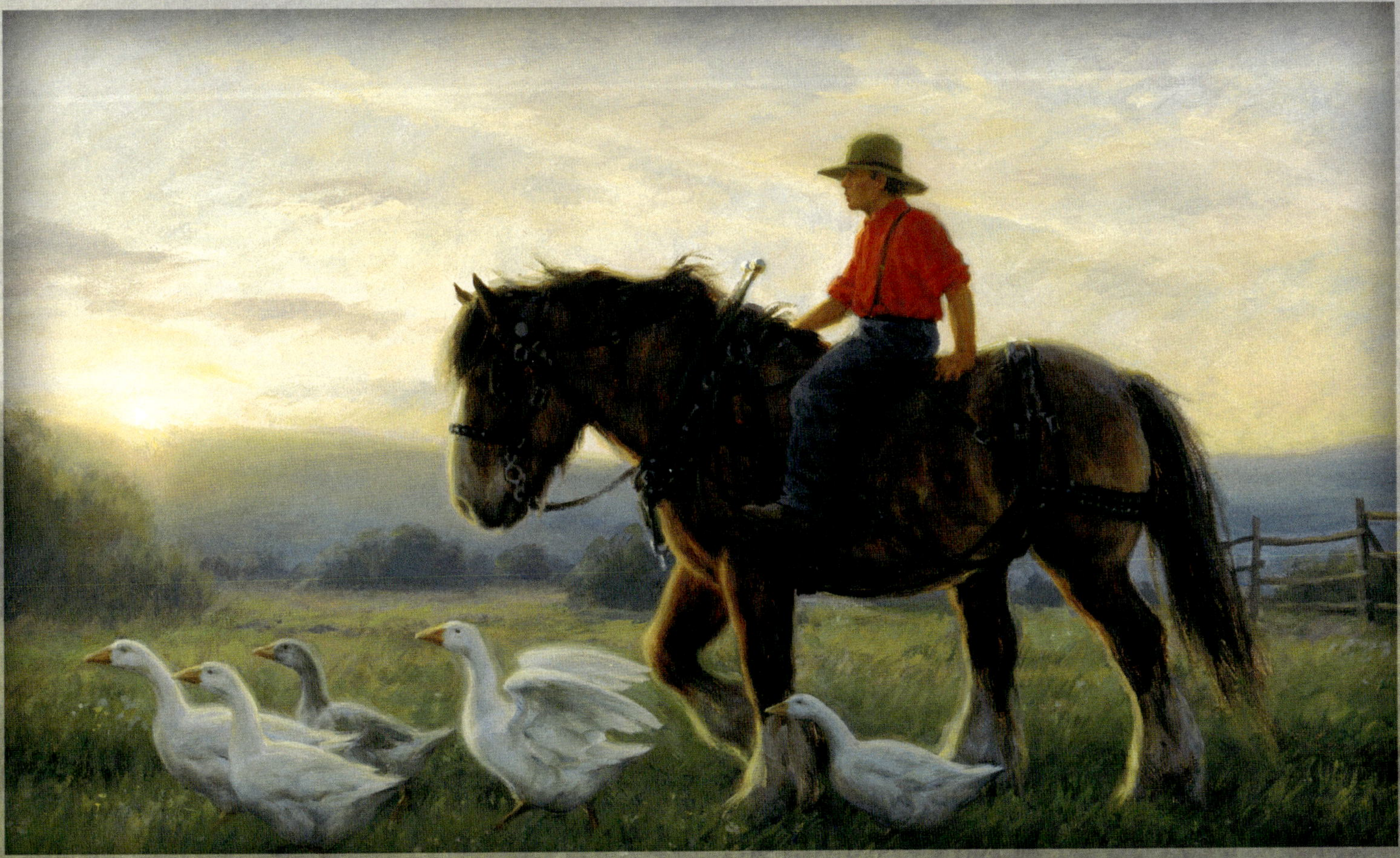

Daddy Clarence was a big man, big not only because I was little. He was bigger than most men. He was a blacksmith. His arms had gotten huge from the many years of swinging a hammer. He wore faded blue coveralls. I guess he was old, but it never seems so.

Once he got the car moving, he tied the reins to the car. He came forward and walked to the side of old Jane and me. I remember feeling warm all over. I was going to spend another summer in a place where there was no time. There was night and day, but days of the week, months and such didn't seem to exist in this green valley tucked in the foot of the mountains.

The ranch was now coming into sight. I could see the puffy clouds marching overhead like columns of soldiers from a story book. The sun was low and already making periodic appearances between the tall poplar and pine trees that circled the house. The corral was always the first thing you noticed upon seeing the place. It was built to last forever, just like everything Daddy Clarence built was meant to do. The corral was made of logs laid on top of one another. It was a great place for sitting and watching, which is what I often did in the mornings and evenings during milking time.

As we were pulled into the ranch, Daddy Clarence turned and spoke to my folks. "You kids go in the house and say hello to Mama Violet. Ronnie and I will turn the horses loose and go cut some meat for dinner."

Mama Violet was grandma. She had gotten the "Mama" in front of her name to match the title we'd given Grandpa. I could smell the sour dough biscuits baking. I was anxious to get that meat cut and begin the final of the two daily meals served at the ranch.

We unhitched the team of horses from the Chevrolet. Daddy Clarence let me hold the reins while he held the harness tree off the ground. Old Jane and Maude knew the routine, so I didn't need to do much guiding. When they arrived at the granary, they both stopped without any cue. Daddy Clarence had always said horses were a lot more reliable than people.

While he pulled off the harnesses and hung them on the weathered wood of the granary, I remembered my job from last summer and rushed to get two buckets with a little bit of grain in each one. I set them in front of Jane and Maude. They eagerly went to eating. I always liked the smell of horses. Daddy Clarence would always say that other animals stink some, but horses just enrich the air.

I was watching the grain disappear from the bottom of the buckets when Daddy Clarence said, "Ronnie, come and look at this." I walked to the side of Ol' Jane and could see Daddy Clarence standing directly under the big, old workhorse. He was crouched down with his back under her belly. "Tell me when all four feet are off the ground."

Then to my utter amazement, he put his hands on his knees and lifted up. All four of Jane's feet left the ground at the same time. It was almost as amazing to see that Jane didn't put up any fuss. She knew Daddy Clarence well. And she seemed to know what the rest of us knew. He never a purpose hurt anything.

Daddy Clarence was strong, really strong. Ol' Jane dangling there in the air was about as much testimonial to that strength as a person could ever ask. Daddy Clarence merely laughed at my amazement. In all the years that followed, I never did hear him say anything about being able to lift Ol' Jane to any one. I have wondered if he simply did it as a way of expressing to me that he could take care of things. When a man has that kind of knowledge within himself, he doesn't need to express it to anyone.

Taking care of horses always came before anything else. Daddy Clarence would say, "The animals eat before you do." And he followed that rule religiously. He loved animals… sometimes more than people…at least some people. Once the horses were taken care of, he placed his big arm on my shoulder and said, "We best go get that meat for dinner, or both you and I will be under Mama Violet's thumb for a good while."

He proceeded to swing the giant corral gate open for us. I preferred to climb the log fence and jump down beside him. Other adults could, just as likely, have scolded that kind of silliness. Daddy Clarence seemed to understand a kid's mind.

The sun was now behind the western mountains. The sky was turning different shades of orange. We both stopped and watched the color of the sky for a time without talking. We had work to do, but Daddy Clarence always said that an important part of life was to do some heavy duty looking. And that's what we did for a long moment.

"Pretty nice, don't you think, Ronnie?"

He looked at me and my smile was all the answer he really wanted to his question. We walked slowly through the barnyard. The chickens were gathering to their roost. You could see the softness of the dust under your feet where they had scratched it loose searching for lost kernels of wheat. The red soil was light and was easily given to creating dust. I watched as Daddy Clarence's boots poofed a little cloud with each step.

About a hundred yards beyond the barnyard was a small stream. It was called Number Five. Not a very romantic name. It was, in fact, part of a series of canals that had been dug by Daddy Clarence and the other early settlers to the valley at the turn of the century. Along the stream were stands of poplar and cottonwood trees, plus clumps of willow. It was in the top of one of those trees that Daddy Clarence would hang the meat.

We walked slowly, watching our shadows increase in length and the color in the sky darken. We walked passed the old house. It was really a shelter Daddy Clarence and Mama Violet had erected when they first came and started working the ranch. Between the old house and the stream were an orchard and a garden. It was still too early in the spring for life to be showing in the fruit trees. Through the bare branches, I could see a ray of light shining directly on the outhouse. To the best of my memory, it was a three - holer. I guessed that this year I'd move up a notch in size.

As we entered the sheltered grove where the meat was hanging, the mountains extinguished the sun's last ray. The air became steel blue. Daddy Clarence lowered the meat that had been suspended from a treetop pulley.

"This is a great piece of venison, Ronnie. Traded Gib Beebee for it."

Daddy Clarence always got his venison from neighbors, even though he was a crack shot and an avid deer hunter. It was a situation I'd wondered about but never dared ask. "I've been saving the best part of this hind quarter for your arrival. With a little seasoning, Mama Violet can make this the best tasting meat this side of gizzard stew."

"Speaking of which…" Daddy Clarence laughed to himself and I knew a story was coming on. He moved the hindquarter of the venison on to his cutting table, took the meat saw that was hanging on a nearby tree, and began cutting some thick steaks."

"When I was a bit older than you, I was livin' in Bear, Idaho. My Dad took me to meet an old mountain man named Perry Greg. The old guy had lived in the mountains so long he'd forgotten what civilization was like. My Dad and me arrived at his camp late one evenin'. Kinda like now. I was starved. Kinda like you are, I'll bet. Well, Dad and I didn't have any food with us. That was pretty obvious to old Greg. And he says, 'Boys, I ain't bee home for a month. I ain't got no meat much, and no tea, but I can get some fir tea. And I still got some grease up there. He reached up in the tree for his fryin' pan. As he did, I looked at his hands. Ronnie, you never saw a man with hands like Perry Greg. He had scales on his hands like a codfish. Well, he reached up and pulled down this fryin' pan and the grease was all gone, havin' been eaten by magpies and blue jays. And they had clearly left their mark. Old Greg shook his head and said, 'Let me make up some fir tea.' (Now, that's simply bows from off a fir tree that ya steep. Pretty bitter stuff.) Dad looked at me and said, 'What about it Clarence, do you want some dinner or not?' And I said, 'No siree. Be late getting home if we do.'" Daddy Clarence laughed heartily. "So, Ronnie, I want you to know how lucky you are to be sittin' down to some real food tonight."

As we walked back to the house, Daddy Clarence began describing all the things he thought we ought to get to this summer. "I'm hopin' that you're old enough this summer that your Mother will let me take you into the mountains."

"Oh, I am," I said excitedly. Even at the age of six, my memory was filled with stories of Daddy Clarence's mountain trips. It wasn't unusual for him to take a team and a couple of saddle horses and go into the mountains for a month or more in the summer.

"Well, we best let me pick the time to bring it up with your Mom. She probably won't think of you as growed up as you and I know you are."

As we approached the back door, Daddy Clarence handed me the armload of steaks. "We may as well start now showin' 'em your grown-up-ness," he said with a wry smile. He opened the door and the smell of sourdough biscuits baking was almost enough to make me forget my excitement about going into the mountains. I was so hungry I thought I could die. Mama Violet called my name and hugged me to her apron. I was near as tall as her waist. Which I duly noted was a bit more than last summer and would certainly lend some weight to Daddy Clarence's argument.

Mama Violet was a pretty woman. Though she was probably old too, her hair was very black and long. She always wore it braided and tied somehow on her head. But I knew it was long because I had seen it once right after Mom had helped her wash it.

"Ronnie, you get the table set and I'll get these steaks done." Daddy Clarence spoke the orders loud enough so every one could hear. I could tell it was just another bit of preparation in his argument for me going into the mountains with him. I hurried and set the table. Mom and Dad were talking quietly at the table. Dad would be leaving in the morning and we wouldn't see him again, except for a couple of days, through the whole summer. Mama Violet was chopping some onions to fry with the venison. Her eyes were weeping with the task. Daddy Clarence and I were the only ones who seemed happy.

Within minutes, Mama Violet ordered, "Everyone set down. It's time to eat." Daddy Clarence came over with a hot frying pan and served everyone a steak. Mama Violet brought on the mashed potatoes, gravy and two large pans of sourdough biscuits. I ate 'til I couldn't swallow. Then I followed Daddy Clarence's ritual to clean up my plate. We each took a hot biscuit. We cut a large chunk from the mound of freshly churned butter. As it melted in the sour

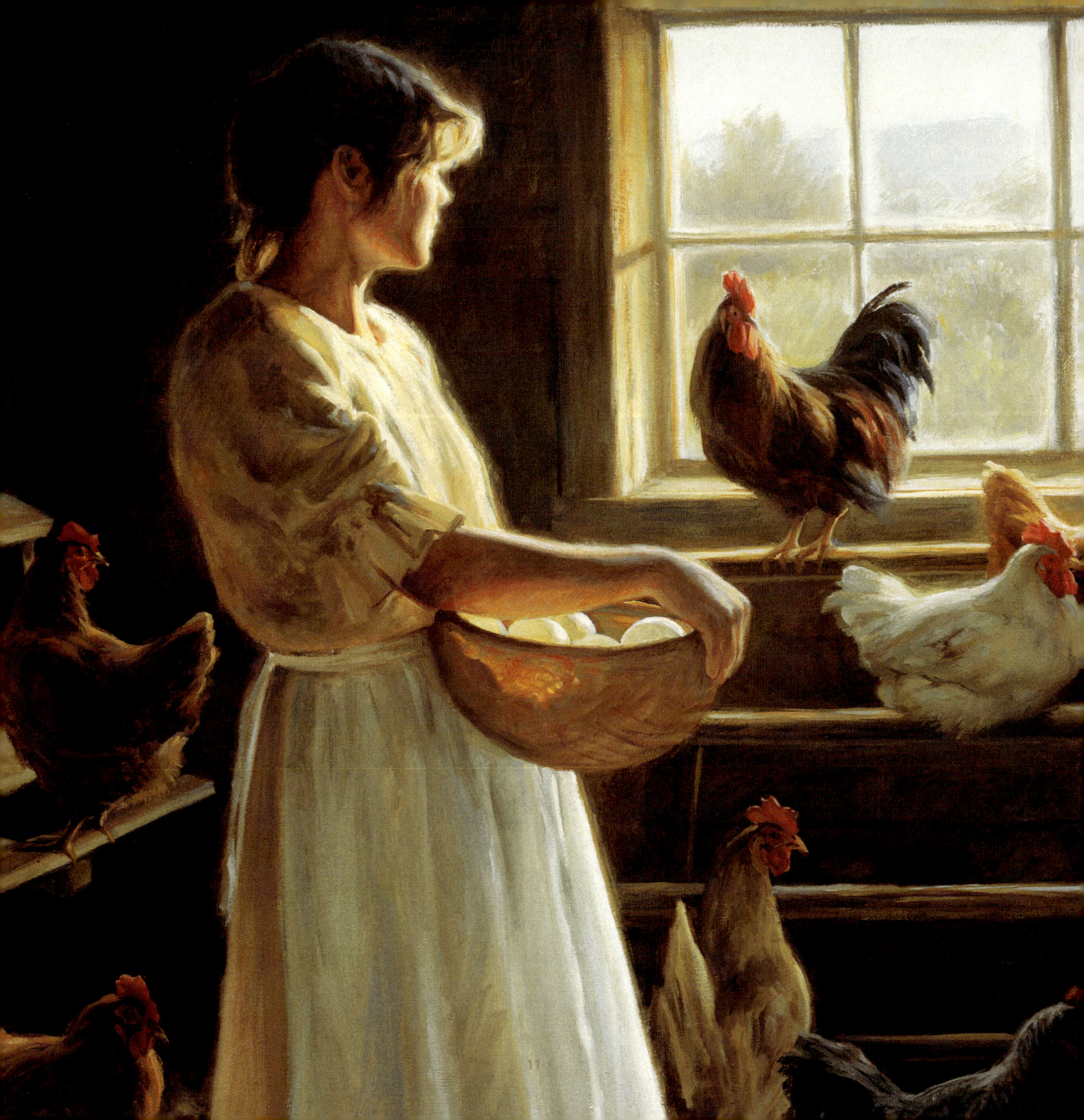

dough, we poured a helping of dark Karol syrup on to our plates. Then we tore off pieces of the biscuit and mopped up the syrup. We left the plates so clean it looked like it didn't matter whether the dishes got washed or not.

With dinner over, Daddy Clarence cleared the table and gave me another job. And he gave it to me loud enough for everyone to hear. "Ronnie, go fill the water bucket, so we can do the dishes." Understanding the larger purpose of the task, I willingly took the shiny metal milk bucket and walked through the newly darkened air to Number Five. I knelt down on a flat rock placed there for that very purpose. I reached out into the bubbling current and pulled the bucket toward me. It was filled nearly to the top. I carried it back much more slowly that I had come. Occasionally the bucket was so heavy, I couldn't hold it away. It would strike my leg and slosh cold water on my pants. By the time I got to the house, there was still a good half bucket left. Daddy Clarence complimented me in front of everyone and set the bucket on the wood stove to heat.

With that, our job was done. Daddy Clarence and I moved into the next room. He lit the oil stove. The air was beginning to chill. I liked the stove. It had a little window in the front, and you could watch the oil flame lick up from the chamber. He sat down in his big rocking chair. I lay on the floor with my chin in my hands and waited for the stories to come.

It was summer. And I was in my own personal heaven again.

Chapter 2

Morning came without me being aware of going to sleep. I awoke with a steel gray light giving outline to the back bedroom window. I could faintly make out the pinecone pattern of the wallpaper. The bed felt so good. It seemed to swallow me. The old quilt, made from the blue denim of worn out overalls, pushed me even deeper into the warmth. I touched my nose and it was cold. I knew that getting up was going to have its price. But I sure didn't want to miss the early morning rituals that I loved to share with Daddy Clarence.

I knew if there was any evidence of dawn in the sky, he would be up. Coffee would be brewing. The crock of sourdough would be overflowing. With great physical effort, I pushed the Levi quilt away from me. I quickly dressed. I knew that moving slowly would only prolong the cold. I entered the kitchen. "Morning, Ronnie. I wondered if you'd hear dawn crackin'." Daddy Clarence's smile warmed the otherwise chilly house. I knew from experience that the cook stove would be the only heat the house would experience till evening. The Depression had etched the use-only-what-you-absolutely-need-ethic deep into every practice of this household.

I watched as Daddy Clarence sat at the kitchen table and poured coffee into his cup till it overflowed into the saucer. He added some thick cream and several spoons full of sugar. He seemed to ignore the fact that the cup was already too full. Once it was mixed he would lift the cup and sip loudly from the saucer. He would then add a bit more coffee, more cream, more sugar. Again, he would sip from the saucer. After repeating that procedure several times, he stood up and walked to the crock of sourdough.

He swung open a cabinet door that had a curved metal bin full of flour. His big hand scooped out a handful of flour and scattered it in a thin layer across the top of the counter. He reached into the crock and pulled out all of the sourdough except for a bit of starter.

He threw the sticky dough on to the flour and with both hands kneaded the flour into the dough. With a couple of pushes from the back of his hand, he soon had the dough so it could be handled. He then squeezed little balls of dough with his thumb and finger. He placed them in a pan near the cook stove to rise. All this was done in silence, though he'd occasionally look at me and smile.

"Evenin' is made for talkin'. Mornin' for listenin'," he'd often say. With the sourdough rising, he went back to the coffee that was now cool in his cup. He downed the whole thing in one gulp.

"The animals are waitin', Ronnie." With that we went out into the cold morning air. He never wore a coat, so that made me feel like I shouldn't either. But, often as not, I would break down and run into the house for mine. I would often marvel at how the cold didn't seem to affect him.

The sky was still dark. The only light was just above the horizon to the east. I knew that would all change in a matter of minutes. It was May. But it was still cold enough to see your breath. The old red rooster was sitting atop the corral fence. With every movement, he would repeat his morning lyric. The horses had gathered from the lower field and were standing together near the blacksmith shop. The breath from their nostrils was creating little clouds.

Daddy Clarence swung open the gate. I followed him in this time. I was not quite awake enough to repeat my climb of yesterday. The first order of business was to milk the cows. I remembered enough of the routine from the previous summer that I walked to the far side of the corral and herded the three cows huddling there toward the barn. Of the three, old Crip was the only one I recognized. Her back leg had been broken several times and mended crooked. She was able to amble along not too far behind the others. One by one each cow walked into the shed. Each knew their place. After they were in, I walked along and slid the wooden stanchion against their necks to hold them in place. Daddy Clarence watched quietly and smiled his approval. I climbed up the corral fence and pulled my coat tight around me. I was hoping my elevated position would attract the first rays of the sun.

"Ronnie, when I was your age I was already milkin' four cows mornin' and night. And I've thought right serious about breakin' you in this summer. But once you've started milkin' the world doesn't seem to let you stop. Milkin' is the only legalized form of slavery left in this country."

Daddy Clarence had his head pressed into the side of the black and white Holstein cow. The rest of him was balancing on a one-legged stool. The cow was chewing in rhythm with the milk hitting the side of the pail. As more and more milk filled the bucket, the streams of milk would sound a deeper and deeper tone. Daddy Clarence's big hands would squeeze one tit, then another. The motion involved being able to squeeze from the top down quickly and surely. It was not the thing that just anybody could start doing. With years of doing it, Daddy Clarence had the motion perfected.

The first light of morning finally broke over the East Mountains.

17

My memory had served me well. The first ray spread its warmth across me like a knife smoothing butter. The light also brought the barnyard cats from under the shed. One by one they lined up at Daddy Clarence's heels.

"Well, look what we have here. You guys decided to make it one more day did you."

Then with uncanny accuracy he squirted a stream of milk into the mouth of each one of them. The cats also knew that there would be milk left in the lid of the old milk can for them after the milking was done. It was their reward for keeping the mouse population to an acceptable level.

"Ronnie," Daddy Clarence was beginning to find his voice. "Thought we might go see Toorroossee today. Do you feel up to a little ride?" He didn't look up, but I could tell by his voice that he was grinning. I knew he wouldn't have brought it up without having cleared it with the folks last night. He was very careful about that kind of thing.

"Which horse do I get to ride?"

"I like the way you say, 'yes', Ronnie. And gettin' the right horse should always be top of one's mind." I knew he would like that. All my life I'd heard him say, " I ain't got much talent for farmin', but put me on a horse and I'll go all day."

I could remember meeting Toorroossee from the previous summer. He was a blind medicine man that Daddy Clarence had befriended. He always had a boy with him that acted as his eyes.

"Soon as we get your Father off, we'll have Mama Violet pack us a little food and we'll saddle up. Your Mom was a little nervous when I told her we'd either be back

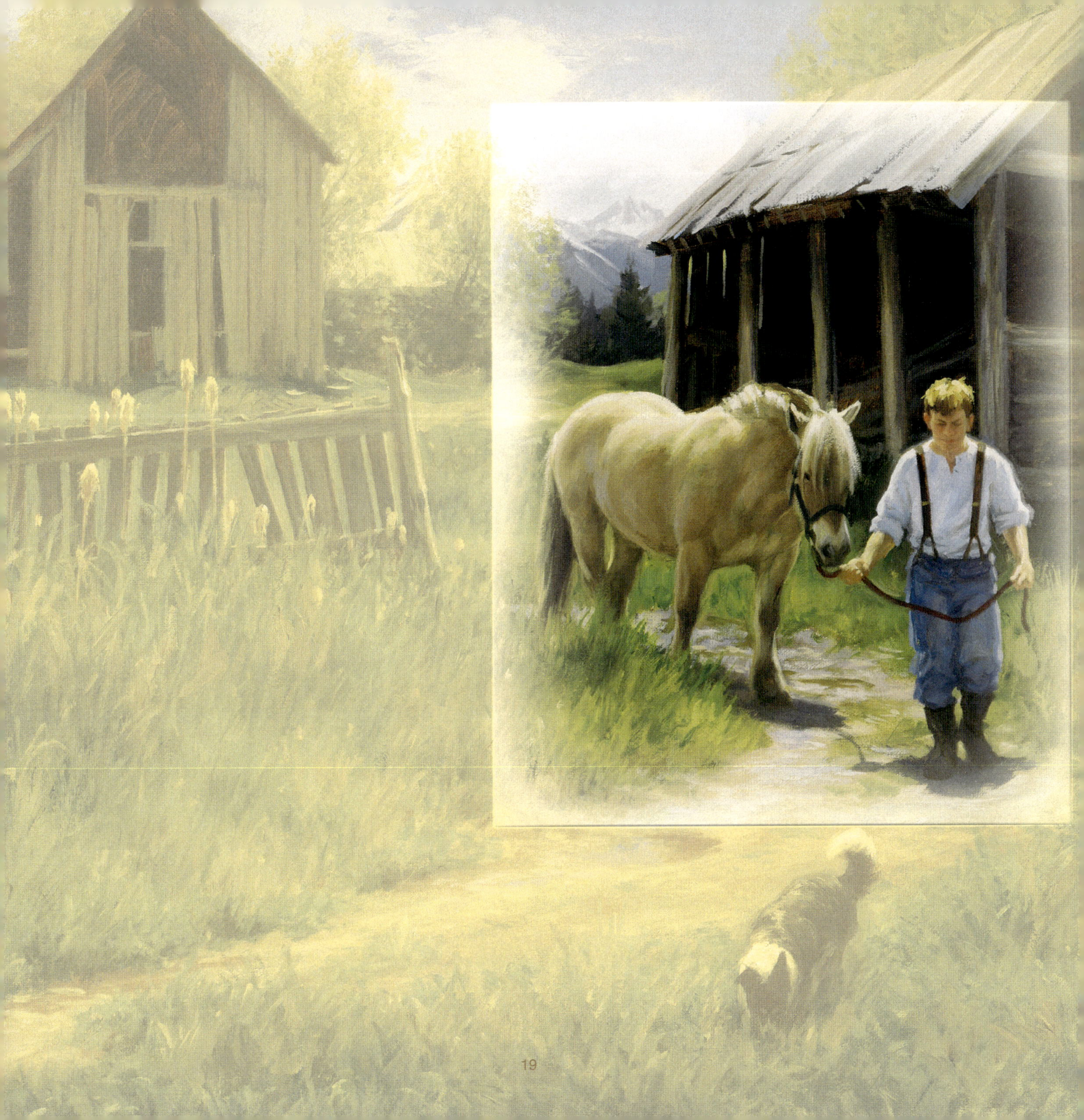

tonight or in the mornin'. But she's lettin' you go. This will be good practice for perparin' her to let me take you into the mountains later this summer."

It was mid morning before Dad left in the forest service truck. We'd get to see him every two weeks for a half-day. Mom was occupied with the baby and she seemed to appreciate that I'd be in Daddy Clarence's care for the most part. Soon as everyone had said goodbye and left, we went to the corral.

Daddy Clarence put a rope on Ol' Rogers, a bay Morgan that he loved as much as his own child. He handed me a bucket of grain and a rope. He told me to keep the rope in the bucket so the horses wouldn't see it. He then set me off to the fields to catch Smokey. Smokey was a horse Daddy Clarence had secured specifically for me the previous summer. I had fallen asleep on his back, ridden every trail on the ranch, and cried when I had to leave him. But I also knew that if I walked into the herd of horses with a visible rope, there'd be a stampede and I'd never catch him.

Smokey was a smallish, blond horse. He may not have been beautiful as horses go, but to me he was the greatest horse in the world. As I walked past the blacksmith shop, I could see Smokey with a group of other horses in the field below the orchard. I called his name. I can't tell you how thrilled I was to see his head suddenly lift from the grass and look my way. I knew instantly that he remembered. But he was still a horse and he wasn't coming to me until Ol' Jane spied the oat bucket and led out.

As the horses crowded around me, I carefully pulled the rope out of the bucket and slipped one end around Smokey's neck. With the other end, I tied a hackamore just like Daddy Clarence had taught me. I folded a loop down, crossing the two strands and pulling the loop through. With the one end still around Smokey's neck, I slipped the hackamore over his nose and the loop up over his ears and led him back towards the corral.

Daddy Clarence was all set. Rogers was saddled and ready. Smokey's saddle was out waiting for me. Daddy Clarence smiled as his eyes examined my hackamore. I could tell he was pleased that I had been practicing over the winter.

"Looks to me like Smokey hasn't forgot. Horses always seem to remember kindness, and they never forget meanness. Do you need help saddlin'?"

I shook my head. Not knowing for sure whether I would need help or not. Last summer I wasn't tall enough to saddle. And I wasn't sure I had grown enough. Daddy Clarence was willing to let me try, so I figured I was up to it. I picked up the saddle blanket. I quickly recognized it as one of Mama Violet's hand-tied-rag rugs that had been folded over. I reached high and got it across Smokey's back. I wasn't tall enough to see on the other side, so I crossed under his neck and straightened it. Then I went to the saddle. Daddy Clarence just stood and watched without giving any advice. I, again, figured he considered me big enough to handle the task. I folded the right stirrup over the saddle seat. Then I did the same with the front and back cinch. With that done I picked up the saddle by the horn and walked over to Smokey. I was barely up to the middle of Smokey's body. I glanced at Daddy Clarence. He still didn't look worried. So I swung the saddle back and then up as far as I could. I was hoping it would stay once I let go.

I was thrilled when it did. I quickly walked under Smokey's neck and brought the stirrup and cinches down. The hard part was over. Quickly I tightened the cinches.

"You may want to walk him around for just a second, then tighten the cinch again. He has a tendency to blow up a bit." Daddy Clarence smiled. I was glad that was all the advice he felt necessary to give me. Once I was firmly in the saddle, Daddy Clarence led Rogers. Smokey and I followed up to the house. Mama Violet and Mom were outside. I gathered they had been watching the whole operation. I was proud that I had gotten the job done. It would serve as proof that I would be capable of going into the mountains later in the summer. Mama Violet was holding a saddlebag full of food. Daddy Clarence took it from her and said, "Thanks, Dearie."

"Now Clarence you be careful with that boy. Don't you do no cowboyin'. He's only six ya know."

Mom reached up and patted me on the knee. I could tell she probably didn't want me to go. "You be careful, Ronnie. You mind your Grandpa."

"I will, Mom." She turned and walked quietly into the house. After just a moment, I could see her standing at the window holding my little brother.

Daddy Clarence swung up on Ol' Rogers. It never ceased to surprise me to see the transformation that occurred when he got on a horse. It was as though years suddenly were taken away from his age. He sat high in the saddle. I could see the excitement in his face.

The sun was nearly straight up when we started out. "We'll probably not be back 'til mornin', Violet. So don't worry none about us." That would mean the evening and morning chores would be done by Mama Violet.

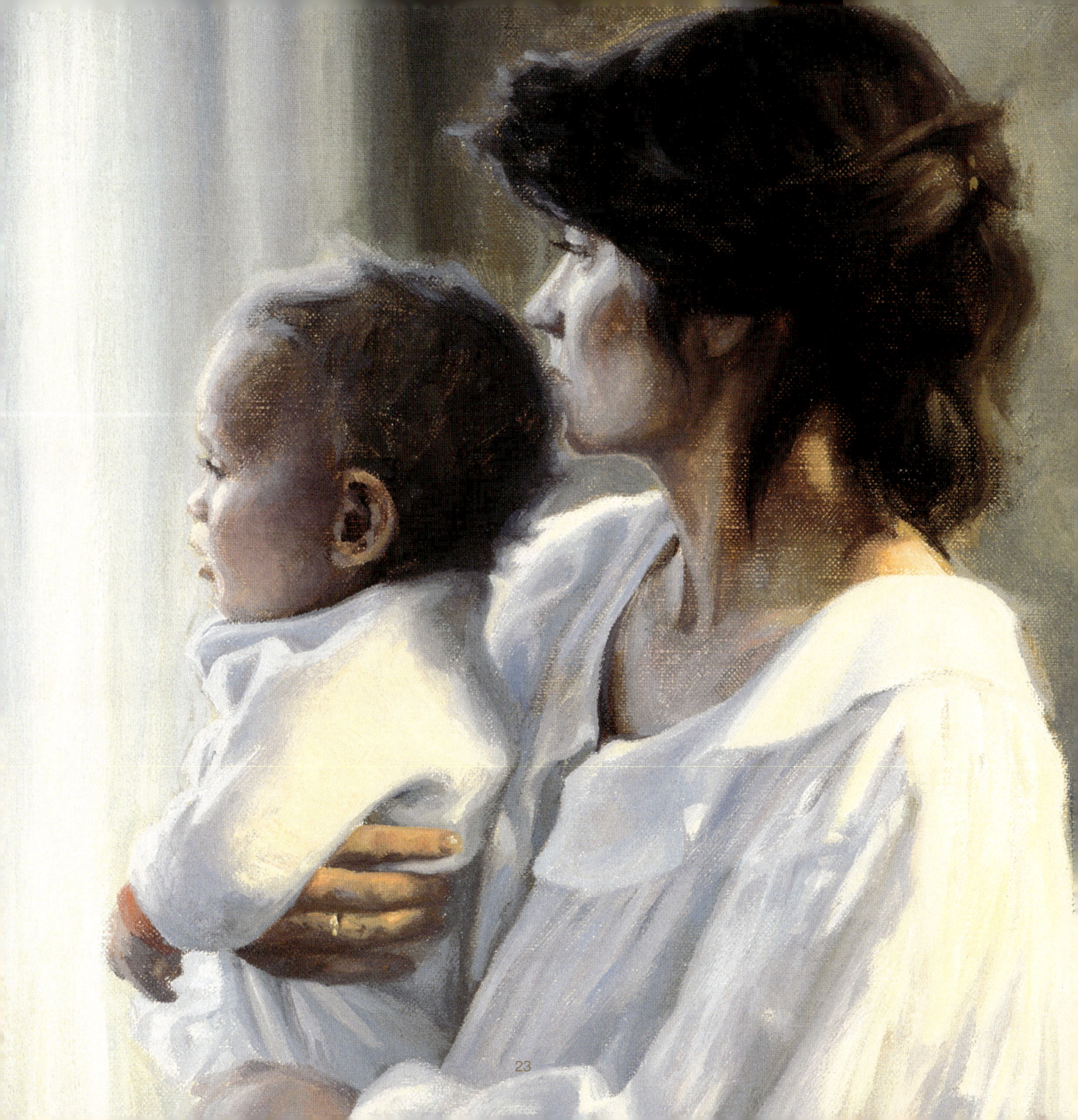

But she never seemed to mind. She looked as happy as Daddy Clarence. She was just happy seeing him happy. You could tell there was something special between the two of them.

Smokey tucked in behind Rogers and followed him head-to-tail. I was in the saddle beginning a two-day ride. I never felt so grown up.

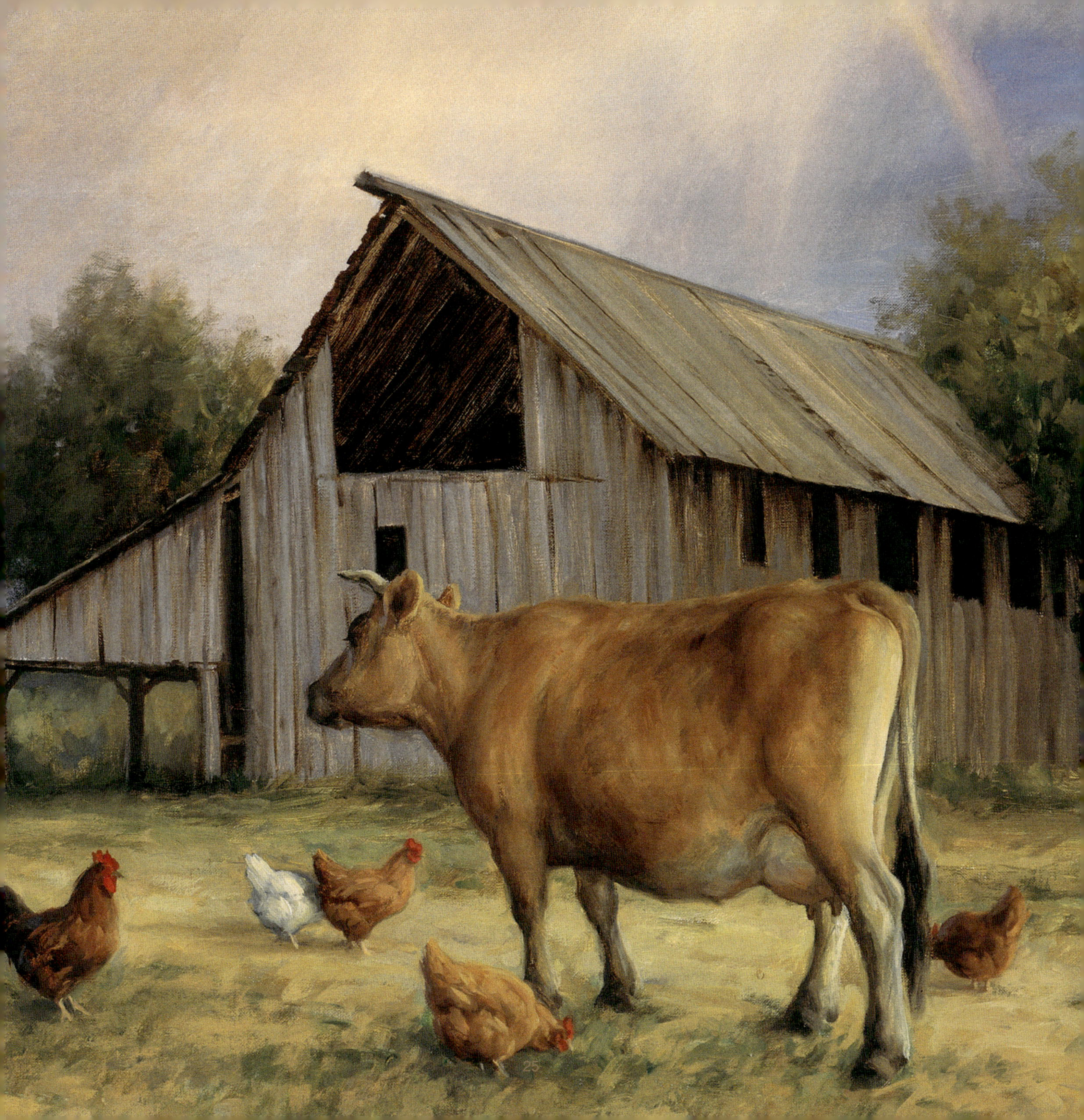

Chapter 3

The warmth of the sun signaled mid-day. It was still early enough in the year that the sun was a smooth, warming feeling that only occasionally licked your face with heat. The red, sandy soil cushioned the freshly shod feet of the two horses. As soon as we passed Number Five, and were out of earshot of the house, Daddy Clarence turned to me and winked. He then moved Ol' Rogers into a canter. Smokey followed.

Before we were too far away, we were into a pretty full run. Daddy Clarence didn't look like any cowboy from the movies with his old straw hat and bib overalls. However, he sat the saddle so smoothly that, if you didn't see the horse under him, you'd think he was sitting on a chair on the back porch. With me it was a little different. I was okay on Smokey, but I was grabbing the horn every time Daddy Clarence wasn't looking. It was just a precaution of course. But it was a fact.

We went for nearly a mile before Daddy Clarence reined in Rogers. Rogers was a bay Morgan. From previous summers I'd remembered the arguments around the fire in the blacksmith shop about which breed of horse was best. Daddy Clarence would scarcely give an inch on his feelings about the Morgans. "They'll go forever," he'd say, "long after every other breed tuckers out." As Rogers started walking out, Smokey had to break into a trot every little bit just to stay close. Finally, Daddy Clarence circled Rogers back and pulled along side of me.

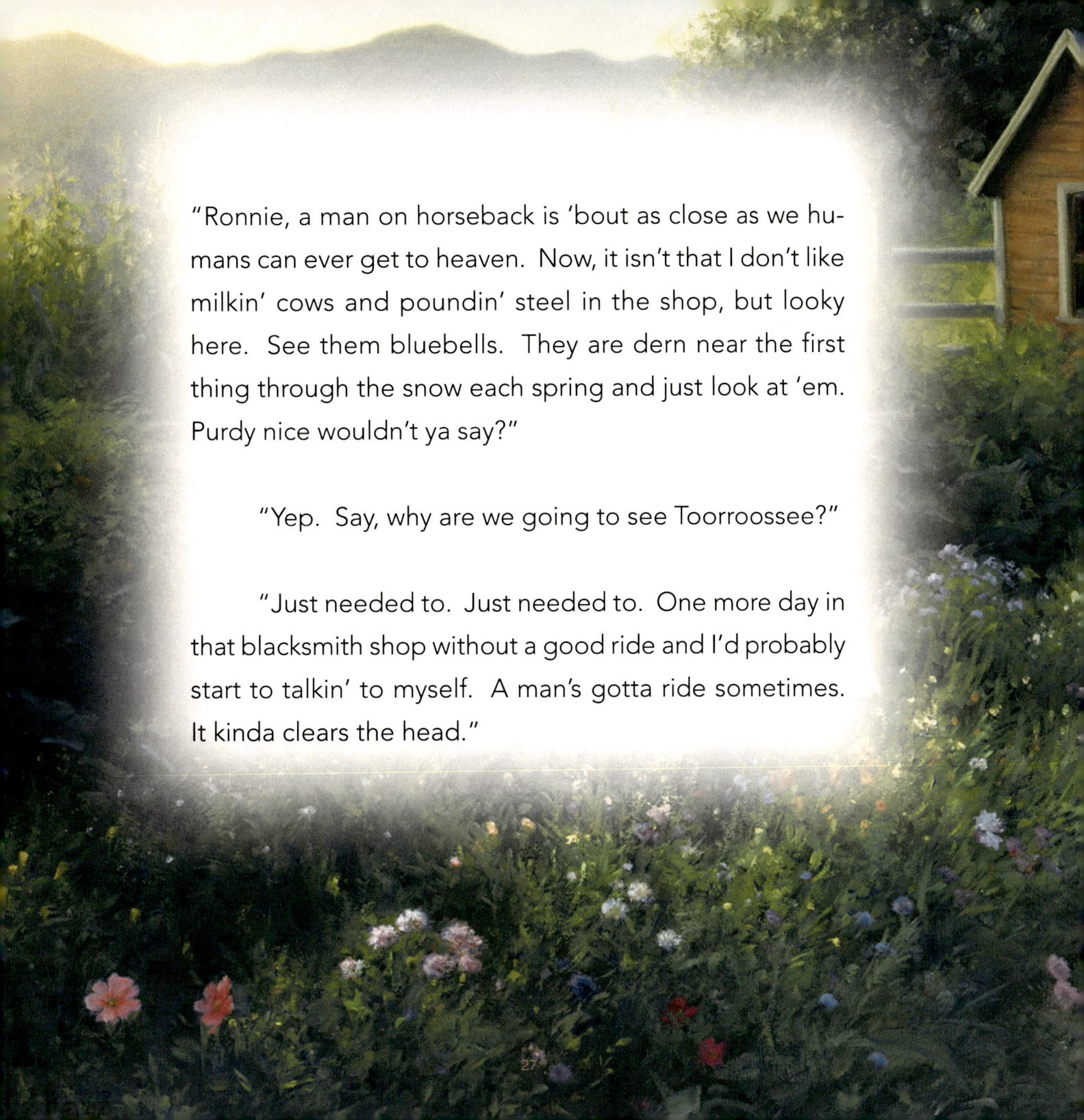

"Ronnie, a man on horseback is 'bout as close as we humans can ever get to heaven. Now, it isn't that I don't like milkin' cows and poundin' steel in the shop, but looky here. See them bluebells. They are dern near the first thing through the snow each spring and just look at 'em. Purdy nice wouldn't ya say?"

"Yep. Say, why are we going to see Toorroossee?"

"Just needed to. Just needed to. One more day in that blacksmith shop without a good ride and I'd probably start to talkin' to myself. A man's gotta ride sometimes. It kinda clears the head."

I got my non-answer, which was what I was hoping for. I knew we'd have a better time if the trip wasn't driven by purpose.

"Ronnie, this here is the ol' Miller place." I looked out at a hillside pasture. "This where them federal guys drove our herd of cows during the Depression and shot 'em."

"Why'd government people do that?"

"We owed 'em 124 dollars and didn't have not one dollar to pay 'em. So they came one day, took our herd of cows, and shot ever one of 'em."

"That doesn't make sense!"

"Didn't mean to make sense. It was meant to make justice. Your Mama Violet is the one it really made angry. Me, it just kinda fit right in to what I've come to expect from government folks.

"Say, looky there boy. If I'm not mistaken, there's a couple of baby owls on that fallen tree over there."

I looked over and could barely see two gray images on the matching gray limb of a fallen aspen tree.

"Riding by in a car, we'd never have seen 'em, let alone been able to pay much attention to the bluebells blooming in the fields. Want you to be careful about traveling too much in a car, Ronnie. You start goin' too fast and you end up missin' most of life."

I reckoned he was right cause even closing in on those owls I wasn't sure what they were until we were almost within touching distance.

"They're just out of the nest. Still can't fly none, but they're near as big as their parents."

Daddy Clarence swung off his horse and dropped the reins in front of Ol' Rogers. Those reins on the ground would keep Rogers in place just as sure as if they had been tied to a cottonwood tree. Daddy Clarence advanced toward the owls. They both tilted their heads this way and that. Daddy Clarence put his left hand in front of one of them. He started wiggling his fingers. While the owl was concentrating on the left hand, the right hand reached around and took hold of the base of both wings.

"Looky here, Ronnie. Just look at those claws. They could pierce a man's hand. And that beak…just look at that!"

He held the owl so close that both the owl and I could see terror in each other's eyes.

"That beak can break bones."

It was with great relief that I saw Daddy Clarence place the frightened owl back on the limb with its nest mate.

"Yep, we'd have never seen 'em ridin' by in a car in a hurry to get some place that really didn't matter much."

He swung back on the horse. Once again, I couldn't help but notice the posture of majesty that seemed to overtake him, natural-like, as soon as he hit the saddle. The road to old Toorroossee's took us passed some beautiful pastures with little streams lazily dividing the green. Willows clustered close to the water. Magpies squawked in protest of our passing from most of the fence posts. We rode for a while in silence. I'd become used to that with Daddy Clarence.

"No better place for a man to get lost than in his own thoughts."

After a bit I could see the outlines of a log cabin on the horizon. "That'll be Toorroossee's place, Ronnie. See that apricot tree right at the front porch. That growed there from one of the pits Toorroossee spit out. It makes gettin' in the door pretty difficult now days."

I could remember a little about Toorroossee from the previous summer. But, as I suspected, Daddy Clarence began reciting the story one more time.

"I met old Toorroossee when we first come to this country, at the turn of the century. All this land sits right in the middle of the reservation. So when the government started selling it off, our neighbors were members of the tribe. Toorroossee was their Medicine Man. He and I hit it off right from the start. But even then it seemed like he was pretty old. Now, of course, he's blind. Stone blind. A few years back when his eyesight started gettin' real bad, he went to a family in the tribe and bought one of their sons to act as his eyes. If my memory serves me correct, he paid 4 sacks of grain for him. Great boy. And he's become a great friend to old Toorroossee."

As we approached the cabin, we could see the boy was saddling their horse. Toorroossee was sitting on a chair. His head was leaning against the cabin wall.

"Clar'nce Smit. I knew'd you'd come."

"How'd ya know it was me." Daddy Clarence looked my way and winked in a knowing way.

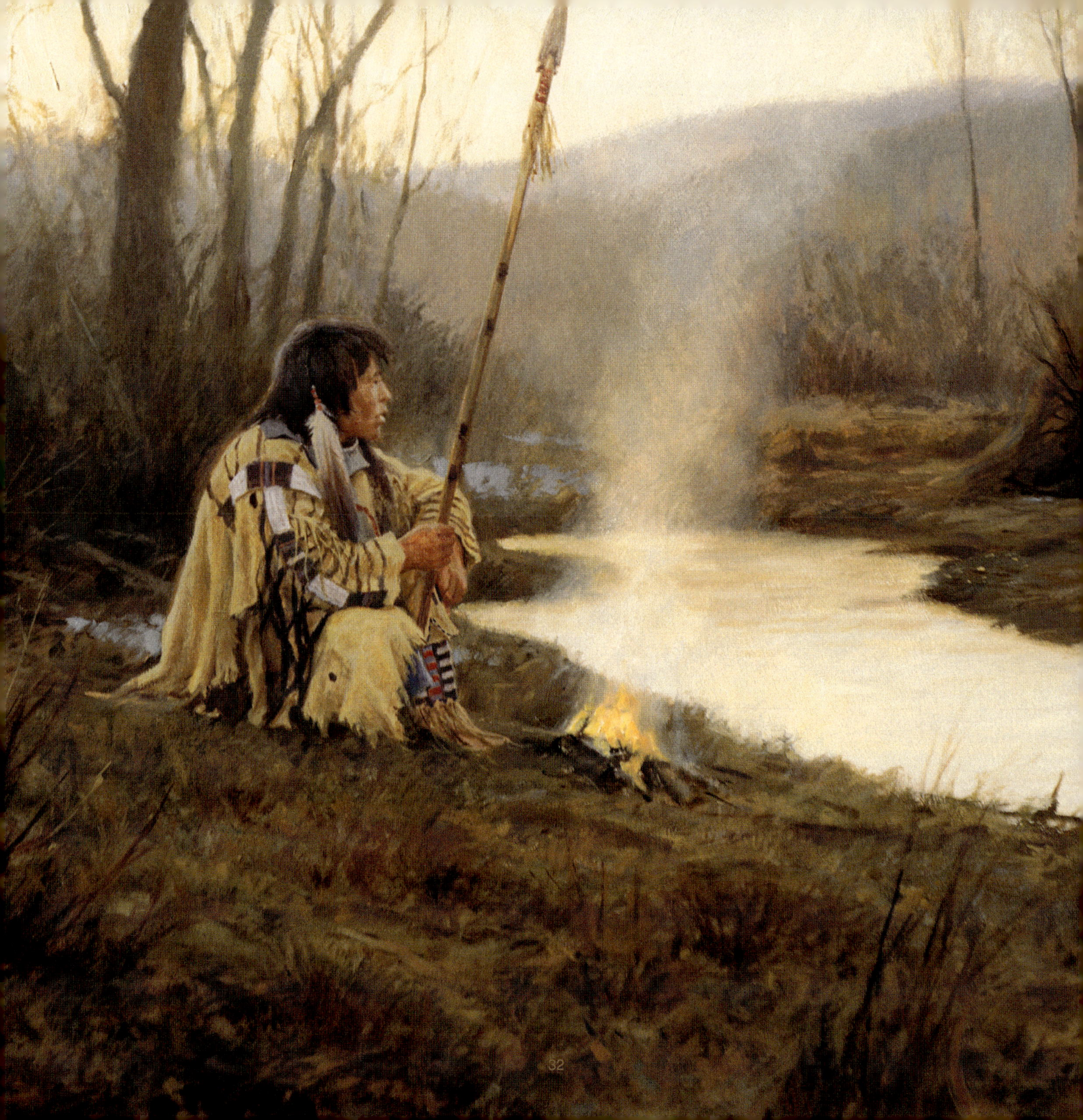

"I may be blint, Clar'nce. But I still got eyes right here." Toorroossee motioned to the boy. I suspected that he was about twice my age.

"Where you headed, Toorroossee? I kin see you're gettin' saddled up for something."

"Well Clar'nce, I go to White Rock to die."

"Tonight?"

"Yes, Clar'nce. Seems like time."

I glanced at the boy. I could see his features tighten with Toorroossee's declaration. He didn't utter a sound, but finished tightening the cinch. I knew of White Rocks. It was the tribal headquarters. Daddy Clarence had told me before how the Indians knew when they were going to die. The women would get out of their sick beds and put on their best dress and make the journey to White Rocks to die.

I didn't know what to make of what had just been said. Daddy Clarence just stood looking at Toorroossee. "You want me to come." It was a statement not a question.

"I tolt the boy that Clar'nce Smit would come."

"We'll ride with you Toorroossee."

Daddy Clarence walked back to me. "Good thing we packed for a couple of nights, Ronnie."

"Did you know he was going to die? Is that why we came?"

"It may be why we came, but I didn't know."

It took me a moment. I could see Daddy could tell by the look on my face that I had figured out what he meant.

"What about Mother? She'll worry if we're late." The words came out before I thought about them.

Daddy Clarence smiled, "Mama Violet has learned over the years that bein' gone a day kin mean most anything. If we're late, she'll know somethin' came up."

I looked over as Toorroossee swung easily into the saddle, hardly looking like a man about to die. The boy climbed on in front of him, took the reins, and turned the paint horse down the road. Toorroossee and Daddy Clarence talked non-stop all the way. Much of their talk centered on the Lost Rhodes Mine. Toorroossee apologized again and again for not taking Daddy Clarence to it before he died. I was a little surprised at how casual Daddy Clarence took the apology after I understood what was being talked about. Toorroossee described a cave with bushels of gold just lying there in its pure form.

"Never been much for gold, Toorroossee. Seen it hurt a lot of folks when I was a kid workin' my way through Nevada. Our friendship wasn't based on you knowin' about no gold."

Each time it was brought up Daddy Clarence would respond in the same way. Each time you could tell that Toorroossee was so pleased that he looked like he was hearing it for the first time.

"You're white Clar'nce Smit, but blood makes us brot'ers."

We approached White Rocks about sundown. Toorroossee had begun to waiver in the saddle. We reached what looked like the center of the headquarters. The boy slipped off the paint horse and helped Toorroossee to the ground. Toorroossee sat cross-legged on the dirt for a moment. Then he bowed his head to the ground. His long white hair hid his face. He chanted something quietly. The boy sat on the ground next to him. Toorroossee reached out his hand and placed it on the boy's head. I could see tears coming down both their cheeks. Daddy Clarence nodded to me, and we rode off to a stand of cottonwoods near a creek just beyond the circle of government buildings.

"Will Toorroossee die tonight?"

"Very soon, Ronnie. He could tell somehow that life was 'bout gone. And he's ready."

We set up a quick camp. I hobbled the horses. Daddy Clarence pulled some jerky and biscuits out of the food sack.

"Tell me about the gold. The mine."

"It's mostly legend, Ronnie. Toorroossee was taken there as a small boy and knowed where it was. He had to know because he was to be the Medicine Man of the tribe. There have been hundreds of men spend their lives lookin' for it and never findin' it."

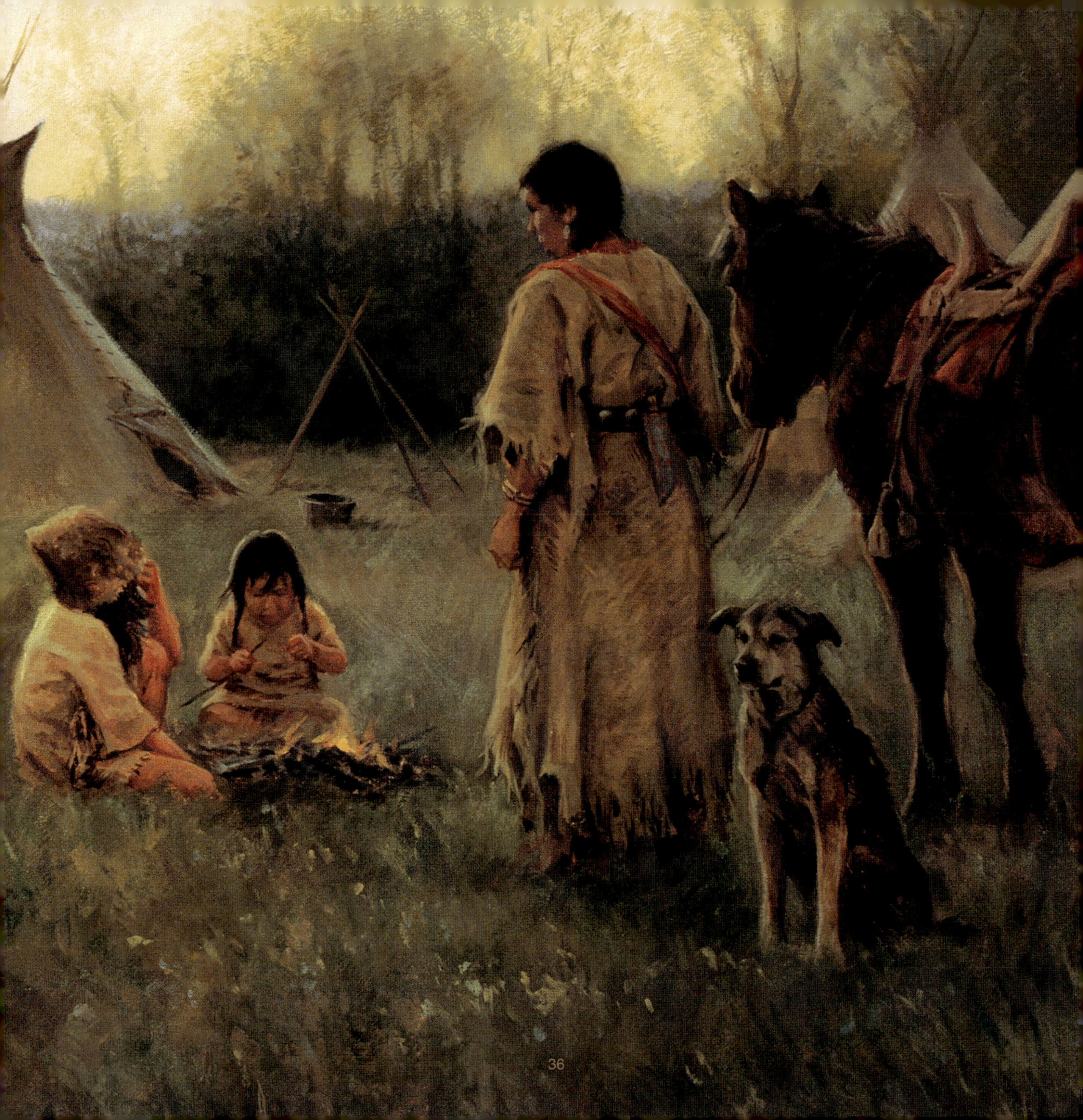

"Why didn't you have Toorroossee take you there before now? Think of all that gold."

"Gold don't buy sunrises…and camps by the creek…and star filled skies, Ronnie. And that's the real wealth of life." As he concluded, drums began to sound.

"Toorroossee has died. We'll go to his burial tomorrow and then head for home."

I looked up in the sky that night. It was dark and black. So black you could almost feel the color itself. I fell asleep before I had many more thoughts. Then at what must have been midnight, I felt a hand on my shoulder.

"Sorry to wake you, Ronnie. But I wanted you to see something purdier than all the gold in the world."

I looked up and the sky was ablaze with stars. There were so many they looked like rivers of white light criss-crossing the sky.

"The wealthy people with the cars and fine houses don't ever see some of the richest sights."

He patted my shoulder. The lesson was given and received.

My nose woke me the next morning. I smelled smoke and bacon both at once. I turned and could just barely see the gray line of light etching the tops of the east mountains. Daddy Clarence had a fire going. I got up to see a breakfast just like the one I had the day before. Daddy Clarence could see the

37

delight and surprise on my face I suspect.

"Cookin' over a campfire shouldn't be no cause for sacrifice."

I was hungry enough that I wasn't about to question. We finished eating about the time the dawn broke full and the drums started. We waited around camp till mid morning. Daddy Clarence cut some willows from the stream and fashioned me a whistle. He carefully removed the green bark. He then replaced it after the channel was cut for the air to pass through.

When the drums finally stopped, Daddy Clarence said, "It's time for us to ride over. They'll be burying Toorroossee now. We saddled up and tied on bedrolls behind us. We rode to the ceremonial grounds. They were a mile or so from the headquarters buildings where we had left Toorroossee the night before.

As we approached, there was a huge crowd of people all standing in a circle. We drifted through an opening and sat on horseback as they placed Toorroossee's body in the burying place. I could see the paint horse lying there still. There was a rifle, food and some other things that were all wrapped up. I gathered these were all things he would need in the world of spirits. I looked across the circle and saw the boy. His face was stained with tears. Then all of a sudden, he burst from the edge of the circle and ran to Toorroossee's body. He screamed something that I couldn't understand. It was the first I'd heard him speak. The men standing by pulled him away. He struggled free and clung to Toorroossee and screamed again what seemed the same words.

I could see Daddy Clarence's face tighten a little. He touched the edge of his hat as if to bid farewell. He then motioned with his head that it was time for us to go. We walked the horses for some time in silence. It didn't seem right to say anything, but finally I spoke, "Daddy Clarence, what was that boy saying?"

Daddy Clarence nodded as if he knew the question was coming. "The boy said, 'Toorroossee will need to see. Toorroossee will need to see.'"

Daddy Clarence looked at me and could see my mind racing.

He channeled my thoughts for me, "Toorroossee learned a lesson from bein' blind. He learned that we all need help seein'. You see, Ronnie, drivin' past bluebells in a fast car can be a form of blindness." I knew he was right.

I knew he was right.

Chapter 4

We got back to the ranch in time for milkin'. Mama Violet asked about Toorroosse and I could tell by her eyes that she was sad.

Come the next morning, some people came by to get their horses shod. I followed Daddy Clarence to the blacksmith shop. It was a clapboard building attached to the southeast corner of the corral. On the south of it, was a pile of iron. The undiscerning eye might have thought it junk. However, to Daddy Clarence it was the raw material for making all kinds of marvelous things from horseshoes to wagon springs.

Daddy Clarence started the fire in the box. As how this was the year that I could help, I was assigned to the blower. It was a three-legged contraption with a handle to move the fan. The faster you turned it, the more air was pumped into the fire, and the hotter it got. I loved turning the fan and watching the coals grow brighter. Daddy Clarence would put a piece of metal in and cover it with the coals. In a very short time, the iron itself would glow with heat. He'd grab the iron with tongs, lay it on the anvil, and shape it with an array of hammers.

The blacksmith's art required you to work quickly before the metal cooled. If you weren't proficient, you could spend your entire time heating metal or pounding cold steel. Both of which were poor uses of time. Daddy Clarence's blacksmith shop was the only real gathering place in the area. He worked in it when people showed up. If they didn't, there were enough other things to fill one's life. He often worked for a "hindquarter of venison, come fall," or some other such arrangement. None of these things were ever written down. Yet I heard him say on more than one occasion, "no man owed him anything".

This day the fire created a warm glow on the faces of Pete Wall and his son. They had come in hopes that Daddy Clarence could shoe their team of horses. Pete Wall needed to plow his north forty while the soil was still moist from the spring thaw. His team was two large black horses with white blazes on their faces.

Their feet were bigger than the span of Daddy Clarence's hand, which is what he used to approximate the size of the shoes he'd need to make. It took nearly all morning to make the eight shoes, but no one seemed to mind the passage of time.

Pete Wall was a quiet sort of man. He seemed kind and appreciative of the quality of work Daddy Clarence did and was doing. He had a small son with him. I thought him to be about four years old. In spite of the many times he was cautioned, he finally ended up putting his fingers into the fan of the blower and getting one of them pretty bloodied.

"Come here, son."

Instead of being scolded at the foolishness of the act, Daddy Clarence's voice was understanding of the curiosity that had provoked the problem. "Ronnie, there's a box of alum above the door there, could you bring it? Let's see if we can draw out some of the pain and stop the bleeding."

Within a few seconds, the boy was quiet. The father's embarrassment subsided. The business of making shoes continued. As he placed the iron in the forge, I was to turn the blower to increase the heat. As I did, I watched the sweat glisten on the face of Daddy Clarence. His big arms, bare to the shoulders, had little rivulets of perspiration making channels down to his elbows.

"Pete, these shoes will last you 'til winter. I guarantee that. They're made of spring steel from that old Model A out back. I'll be pullin' these long before you find 'em wearin' out."

Pete nodded his head. "I know, Clarence, everthin' yous makes lasts."

Daddy Clarence smiled at the compliment, looked in my direction, and winked. That was the best pay you could give him. The talk drifted to all sorts of subjects…from horses to foot races to winter skiing. Sometime after the sun reached its high point, Daddy Clarence took some oil from a can that was tucked into the corner of the shop. He dabbed it on the feet of the team to make them shine. He then called the job finished.

"Much obliged, Clarence. I be getting' you paid as soon as the creamery check comes in the next week or so."

"I know you're always good for it Pete."

"Well, Ronnie, holdin' up those feet of them black Belgiums has me about tuckered out. What say we go relax a bit before Mama Violet makes us come in for supper?"

I nodded my approval.

"I've got this place over by the stream that nobody knows about. I'll nod off for a few minutes while you pick some of the wild raspberries growin' there. What do you say?"

We walked past the orchard and through the garden area. Daddy Clarence was still sweating even though the temperature was mild. At the edge of the garden, we pushed through some willows and climbed over a barbed wire fence. There was a wooden head gate for turning water and a patch of grass newly greened from spring. Daddy Clarence reached down into the water with both hands and splashed water over his face and arms. The final handful he brought to his mouth and drank deeply.

"Nothing tastes quite as good as good water. And water like this, right out of the mountains, is as good as it gets, Ronnie." With that he pulled off his shoes. He leaned against the trunk of an old cottonwood tree that had been growing there for years, living off that good water. His eyes closed. But he kept talking.

"I've been thinkin' about us goin' into the mountains come July. I figure that will give me time to convince your Mother and Grandmother that I ken tend ya okay. The mountains is a great school, Ronnie. Now it don't replace book learnin', but it sure helps make the book learnin' bearable."

"Did you like school, Daddy Clarence?"

"I suppose I didn't give school a fair chance, boy. I went summers for a while in Idaho before my parents split up. But it was so hot, and I was wishin' so bad to be on horseback in the mountains somewhere, that school and I jest never really hit it off."

"What was your life like when you were my age?"

"Well, I lived in a place called Bear, near the Salmon River. My folks were doin' the best they could. Dad was drivin' a team for a mining company and Mom run the post office. I did everything I could on horseback. Dad was into drinkin', and Mom and I didn't get along all that well. Guess that's where I learned to enjoy bein' in the mountains by myself. I kinda figured a man ought to make his self the best company that he can be in."

"I was left to wander on my own after I was 14. Picked up blacksmithin' in the gold fields of Nevada. Drifted to a little place in the mountains near Park City. I smithed for a crew building a tunnel to drain the silver mines. Met up with Mama Violet. And to be real honest, that's when I started my life for real. She's the best thing that ever happened to me, Ronnie."

"Don't copy my life, boy. Your Dad has an education and it's a good thing. Bein' a teacher is a stable life. And he gets to spend all summer in the mountains. So he's got the best of everything. You take after your Daddy, boy."

"Now, you pick yourself some of those raspberries there by the head gate. I don't know how they got started there, but they're awful sweet…probably the water."

With that his voice trailed off and his body relaxed in sleep. I walked over to the bushes filled with the early raspberries and picked a big red one. It was warm from the sun and the taste was smooth and sweet. I looked at the water rushing through the head gate. It sounded like some lullaby. If you watched long enough, the water carried your thoughts away with it. I could see why Daddy Clarence would come here to relax.

Unable to wait any longer, I pulled off my shoes and peeled off my socks. I reached my foot down to the water expecting it to be icy cold. When the tip of my toe touched the surface, I was not disappointed. The water was right off the snow pack. I couldn't imagine anything being that cold and not being frozen.

It wasn't long before I found myself laying back on the grass and looking at the patterns of light through the cottonwood tree. At some point, I must have fallen victim to the tranquility and drifted off, because the next thing I remember was Daddy Clarence touching my shoulder.

"Mama Violet's going to be calling us to supper any moment."

He smiled down at me realizing that I too had fallen under the same spell he'd come to enjoy in this little grove of trees by the stream. As I walked back, I felt something that was really warm. I wondered how many times in my life I would feel it again.

Almost sensing my thoughts, Daddy Clarence spoke, "A grassy place under a tree, next to a stream, creates about the best feeling a man can have. I often wonder if people with lots of money could find anything that they could buy that would make them feel so good. Of course, I reckon I'll never know." He smiled at me, knowing that he knew.

Supper was chicken and dutch oven potatoes. I suspected that it was one of the older hens from the coop. Often when they quit laying, they would end up on the supper table. The chickens were Mama Violet's rather exclusive domain. I'd seen her in previous summers grab the wings of one of the old hens. She would carry the hen to the chopping block, which was really part of the trunk of a tree that always had a rusty hatchet in it.

Mama Violet would lay the chicken's neck on the block and the next thing I knew the hen would be running around the yard without a head.

Once it stopped running, Mama Violet would carry it to the house where she'd have a kettle of water already boiling on the stove. She'd dunk the chicken in for a bit, pull it out, and then take it outside. There she would pull all the feathers off it. Once it was cleaned, it was ready for cooking. It was a process done with   little emotion. It was seen as part of the living and dying that we are all a part of.

This afternoon the chicken tasted awfully good. The dutch oven spuds were as flavorful as I could ever remember. The biscuits were hot. After supper, Mama Violet noted that we were low on butter. Daddy Clarence seized the opportunity.

"Ronnie's turned into quite a help. I'll bet he could run that churn for ya." He winked at me. I picked up right away that he was using this as another opportunity to show that I was grown up enough to take into the mountains.   I willingly jumped at the task. I pulled the   butter churn off the counter. It was a glass bottle that had a lid with wooden paddles hanging down with a crank at the top. Mama Violet filled it with rich, heavy cream and put me on the back porch to go at the churning.

The churning was easy and tiring at the same time. I traded hands and tried to think of something else other than how long this was going to take. After the longest time, the churning became harder and harder. Soon I could see little bits of yellow…then more yellow. I carried the churn back into the kitchen. Mama Violet and Mother were doing the dishes.

Mother smiled at me and said, "My that looks ready. I guess you are growing up." I felt real good even though my arms ached. I was pleased that I had made more than just butter. I watched Mama Violet dump the contents of the churn into a bowl. She then took a wooden paddle and pushed the yellow butter together, squeezing out the white milk. She poured off the milk and cut the butter into small portions.

I walked back out on the porch and Daddy Clarence was whittling a piece of cedar wood to, what looked like, no particular end. "So, I overheard the women folk praising your growin'-upness." I nodded. "The trip to the mountains may just work out."

As he spoke, I saw a figure with a tall black hat enter the barnyard. Before I could ask, Daddy Clarence said, "It's Long John. He must have smelled Mama Violet's chicken.

He's deaf and dumb, but he's real good at smellin'."

Long John was fittingly tall. His deep brown skin took on a golden tone in the failing sunlight. Daddy Clarence waved to him and spoke. Long John simply nodded. He held a rope in his hand. He had a loop in the end. He worked it one way then another in front of him. "Ronnie, run in the house and get Mama Violet and your Mother. Long John would like to earn a little supper."

Mama Violet came out of the house immediately. Mom followed carrying my little brother. They walked to the fence and watched with some anticipation. Daddy Clarence said quite loudly, though I was certain even then Long John couldn't hear him, "Okay, you've got your audience."

Long John smiled, took his rope, and began twirling it in a circle in front of him. The circle of rope became bigger and bigger as he fed more and more rope into the loop. Soon he began to step in and out of the circle. Then he jumped into the circle and made a huge ring around himself. Everyone, including me, applauded. He then threw the rope high into the air. The show was over. And a show it was.

Mama Violet walked over to him and grabbed his arm. She said in a quiet voice, "I'll bet you'd like a chicken sandwich." Long John nodded his head. I couldn't figure out how he was able to hear her. But then I guess he understood her. Usually, that's better than hearing anyway.

Daddy Clarence walked over and picked up Long John's rope. He began to make a circle of his own. He could only make a small one and then it would fall apart. "Come here, Ronnie. See if you can do this."

I picked up the end of the rope and made a small loop. Daddy Clarence stood behind me and took hold of both my wrists. At the right moment, he began to make a circular motion with my hand. For a second or two we made a spinning loop. "Guess you and I'll never make it on the supper circuit. Long John and Will Rogers won't be threatened with anything we can offer."

Mama Violet walked out of the house with the biggest chicken sandwich I'd ever seen. Long John ate it faster than I'd ever seen anything eaten. It wasn't but a moment before Mama Violet was back with another one. Long John smiled broadly and took a bit more time on this one. He, then, went out and picked up his rope. The sun was all but down. He spun one more loop in front of him and then turned it perpendicular to the ground. Soon the loop was as tall as he was. He began jumping through it, first to one side then the other. He stopped amidst the clapping of hands, tipped his hat, turned, walked silently out the gate and up the road.

The dimming twilight was off set by the rising of a full moon. Its pale light and the warming spring air kept Daddy Clarence and I out on the porch well into the dark. Mostly we whittled, but occasionally there were words.

"You know, Ronnie, there's a lot of talk about the man in the moon. But my Father showed me the face of a woman in the moon. That's all I see any more when I look at it." He then took his hand, the one with the knife in it, and pointed to the moon. He brought his arm next to my head so I could sight along it. Then he traced with the point of the knife, the face of the woman. Sure enough there it was, a woman's face.

"Now, Ronnie, I don't know if there's any truth to it, but the old timers used to say that if the face of the woman is ever looking directly down, you're about to have a rainstorm that will beat all get outs. Now I've only seen that happen once. It was in the mountains, but that storm nearly took a whole mountain side with it."

I was whittling a long stick trying to make a handle in it. Daddy Clarence was simply making shavings. He looked at my work and asked, "What you got goin' there?"

"Nothing."

"Sometimes 'nothing' makes the best of all things. Let me see."

He took the stick. I had stripped the bark off it, so it was smooth and moist. In one end there was just enough indention to call it a handle.

"Looks to me that you've got the perfect toy."

"Really?"

"Well, yes. It's a sword. A walkin' stick. A bat." The list went on, and with each mention he made a motion that turned the stick into the item. When he finished, I had to quite agree. It was the perfect toy. It could be anything. I went to bed that night and took my stick with me. It had become my most precious possession. Through the rest of the summer, my stick was never far from me. I lay in bed holding my "sword" fighting the air that was clouded with bad knights from some medieval realm…'til I heard thunder.

A storm began hammering the window. In the midst of the late night lightning, my "sword" gave me the courage to climb out of bed and go to the window. I parted the drapes to see if I could see the face of the lady in the moon. The clouds were too thick. As I went to sleep with the rhythm of the rain on the window, I decided she must have turned her face downward.

Chapter 5

The next morning you couldn't help but notice the freshness left in the air from the thunderstorm. The sandy soil had welcomed the moisture. The newly green trees glistened with the jewels of water each leaf was displaying to the morning light. The chores went quickly. Daddy Clarence seemed to be in some particular hurry. As soon as the milking was done, he announced the plan for the day. "I thought you and me might ask Mama Violet about us ridin' over to the Yellow Stone and visitin' Jesse."

Breakfast was barely out of the way when Daddy Clarence gently broached the subject of us going to the Yellow Stone. "Violet, I was thinkin' that Ronnie and I ought to pack up some shoes and tools and go and shod Jesse's team. He's gonna start plowin' any day now, and…"

He hardly got that many words out before Mama Violet said, "I figured you'd want to start gettin' closer and closer to the mountains with this weather warmin' and everything. I'll pack you supper and some food for Jesse."

Now the Yellow Stone could be seen from the ranch. It was a large pale-yellow ledge on the face of the mountains some miles away. Jesse, to the best of my recollection, was part Cherokee who had hired on some years before with a rancher by the name of Glen Stevenson. He had the mind of a child. It seemed to me that Daddy Clarence and Mama

Violet had taken to caring for him. I knew him from previous summers. He would always stop by the ranch on his way back from town. He'd leave candy that he'd won at the punchboard games in the pool hall. It was his way of saying thanks for the care he was experiencing.

I had a saddle on Smokey and was waiting for Daddy Clarence to check the cinch before he even came out of the house. Mama Violet was holding on to his arm. I knew she didn't particularly want him to go. However, she became awfully happy seeing how happy even going towards the mountains made him. Behind them, Mom was walking, carrying the baby. I could see she was getting ready her, "Be-careful-and-mind-your-Grandpa speech." I was ready to appropriately say, "I will."

It wasn't but a few minutes and we were on our way. Instead of going east toward White Rocks, we headed west.

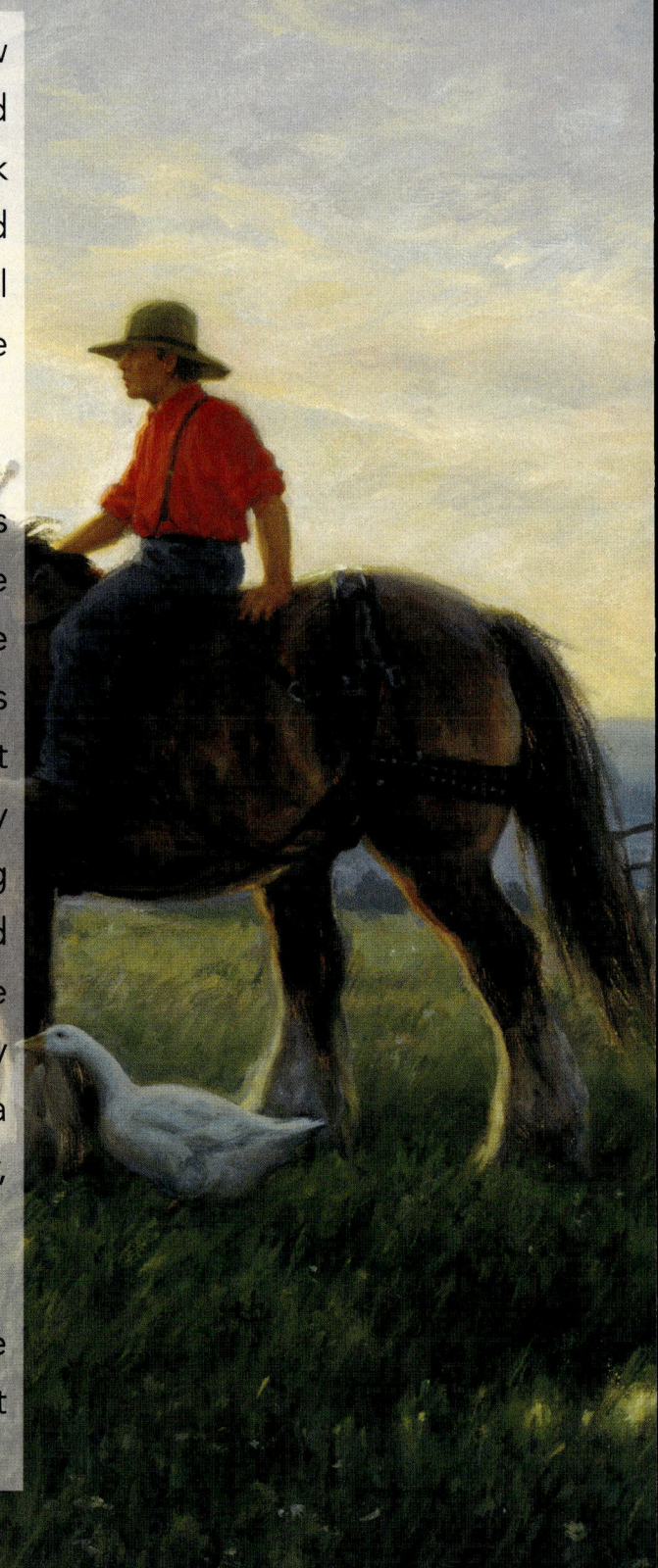

The road was red and sandy making it soft for the feet of the horses. Daddy Clarence led a packhorse on which he had thrown all the stuff Mama Violet wanted him to take to Jesse. A rope tied into a diamond hitch made certain that nothing would come loose. Daddy Clarence knew all kinds of knots. He had taught me many of them. I knew the turk's head, both double and single. I could tie the hackamore which came in awfully handy when you caught a horse in the open field. The diamond hitch was still a ways off for me. Perhaps before the summer was over, I could get the hang of it. We rode west to Gib Beebee's house, then turned north, and headed directly toward the Yellow Stone.

Daddy Clarence broke Ol' Rogers into a gentle lope with the packhorse following. I came behind with Smokey. The horses sensed the sensation of the spring breeze and loved the chance to have it toss their mane. We rode at a gentle, rocking-horse gate for several miles before Daddy Clarence pulled Rogers in. "Ronnie, I believe just across that river there we'd find a pile of arrowhead chippings. Ya game to take a look?"

We crossed the Uintah River without problem. The spring thaw had just barely begun to bring the water down from the mountains. The water level was still fairly low and the current easy. The horses stepped through the water without hesitation, a characteristic of well-traveled, ranch horses. We climbed a steep bluff looking over the river. At the top, Daddy Clarence stopped and swung off Rogers and dropped the reins to the ground. I followed suit and dropped Smokey's reins. The horses nibbled at some tufts of grass that were just starting to green. The sun was midway up the sky and was dancing on the surface of the river below making little diamonds of light.

"Ronnie, looky under that serviceberry bush there. Sometime ago they buried a little Indian baby there. I remember Toorroossee pointing that out to me. This is sacred ground, so we won't want to disturb anything. But come here to the edge of this bluff." I walked near him. "Can you see anything unusual?" My eyes scanned the ground. I didn't see anything out of the ordinary. "Seeing things is an art all itself. This pile of rocks is a pile of rocks unless you notice that they are all chips of flint."

I stooped down and saw shiny blue flakes of rock.

"If you sort those chippings carefully, you may just find a broken arrowhead. Sometimes in the makin', one will get damaged and they just leave it."

I sorted the rock chips, trying my best to see shapes. I finally found a very, very small piece that was a perfect arrowhead except that one of the flanges had been broken off. "Look. Look!"

Daddy Clarence just smiled. I realized then, though I didn't say it, that I was simply discovering something he had found before and left for me to discover.

"Those little chippings can tell quite a story. That arrowhead is a piece of genuine history. People sat here years ago on a morning just like this and tried to fashion a piece of rock that would help them eat that evening. Think about that, Ronnie. Things are a lot different for you and me now. But a few years ago, the next meal was about all a man could get done in a day."

I held the broken piece of history very carefully.

"I reckon the spirits wouldn't mind you keeping that, iffen you treasure it."

I put the broken arrowhead in my pocket and looked at it several times in the next hour. For the rest of the day, I found myself touching my pocket to see if I could still feel the treasure. I thought about the man who made the arrowhead. I thought about the work he had put into each careful chipping only to have his hours wasted by one single blow.   It's quite a feeling to touch history. I sensed it that day. I asked

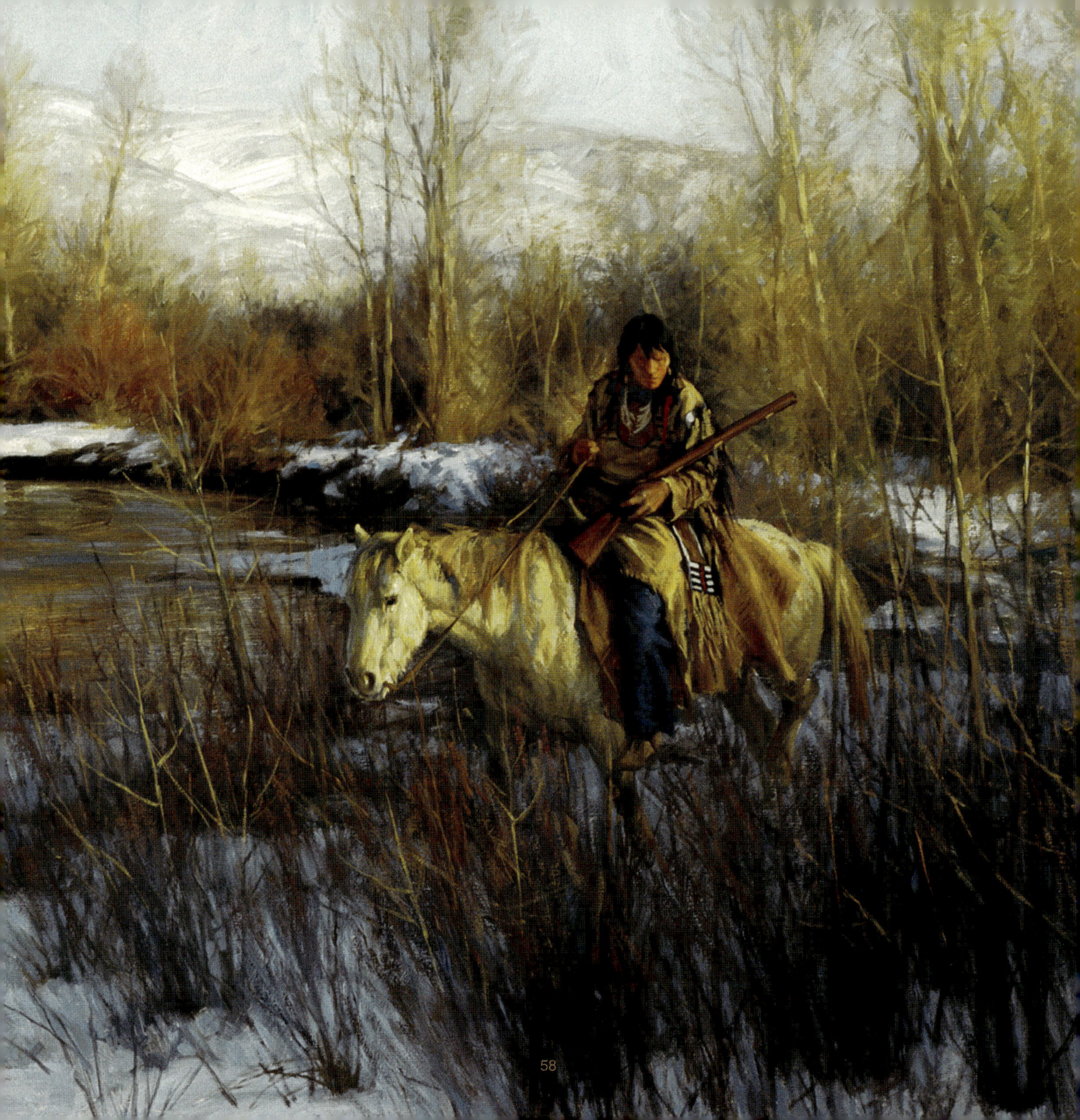

Daddy Clarence about it as we pulled up at a stand of trees near half way to the Yellow Stone.

"It's awe-inspirin', Ronnie, to realize that you are a product of thousands of people who came before you. Every little thing you enjoy was bought, in part, by their sacrifice and pain. That's a pretty heavy thought. I've knowed people who couldn't imagine a God actually existin'. But even the most cynical of all folks has to admit that they owe a heapin' amount of thanks to ancestors. So I'm glad you feel the sense and the wonder of history in that arrowhead. That's a good lesson."

It was nearly evening before we reached the little one-room log cabin nestled against the line of willows. We crossed a small creek where it widened and spread to where it was only a few inches deep. It was obvious that years of running a wagon over the bank and through the stream had caused the spreading. It was a perfect place to water stock, since the widening made the water more accessible. Jesse's place was comprised of a log cabin no bigger than Mama Violet's kitchen. On a little rise above it was a wooden granary. Some fifty-yards from the cabin door was the outhouse. We weren't thirty-feet from the cabin when the ugliest dog I had ever seen in my life lunged out of the granary door. Daddy Clarence looked at my fearful expression and smiled, "I forgot to tell you about Watch."

"Watch?"

"Watch...dog."

I laughed. "What happened to his face?"

"Met up with a hay mower as a pup. Cut his nose plum off. He was so hurt and so ugly they was gonna shoot him 'til Jesse happened a long. Jesse never met an animal he didn't like. Ol' Watch will become mild as a kitten soon as Jesse comes home. And from the looks of the sun dropping, that should be any minute. So we had best just stay on the horses for a bit. 'Cause, without Jesse, he's about as mean as he looks."

We sat on the horses until a wagon piled with hay came out of the draw to the west of the cabin. The hay wagon was being pulled by a team of sorrel horses. As it approached, Daddy Clarence filled in the blanks that were in my mind as to exactly why we were here. Other than, of course, it was ever closer to the mountains.

"Jesse's nigh onto forty years old. He's a half-breed, half-Cherokee. And he's got the mind of a child. He's as kind as they come. He just kinda happened along one day. He's a good worker. We got this home built for him. He helped with most of it. And he worked off the cost of most everything by working Glen Stevenson's place. And he's just kept on workin' for Glen since then. Mama Violet kinda took on the lookin' after part for the community from that time on."

Jesse pulled into the yard and stopped his team. Daddy Clarence swung off Rogers. I glanced at Watch. He immediately had his tail, or what was left of it, wagging as fast as it could go. He almost looked presentable compared to the mass of ugly flesh he presented not more than two minutes before.

"Looks like you got a good load there, Jesse."

Jesse smiled without saying a word. His mouth had several gaps where teeth used to be.

"You remember Ronnie, here?"

Jesse looked at me and nodded.

"Let us help you with that hay."

I stepped off Smokey at that point, careful to check that Watch was still the mild pup he had suddenly turned into. Daddy Clarence and I sat on the rear of the wagon and let our feet dangle while our backs nestled into the hay. After all day in the saddle, it felt mighty restful. The hay smelled warm and sweet. The corral was just a ways up the road to the East. We were there in minutes.

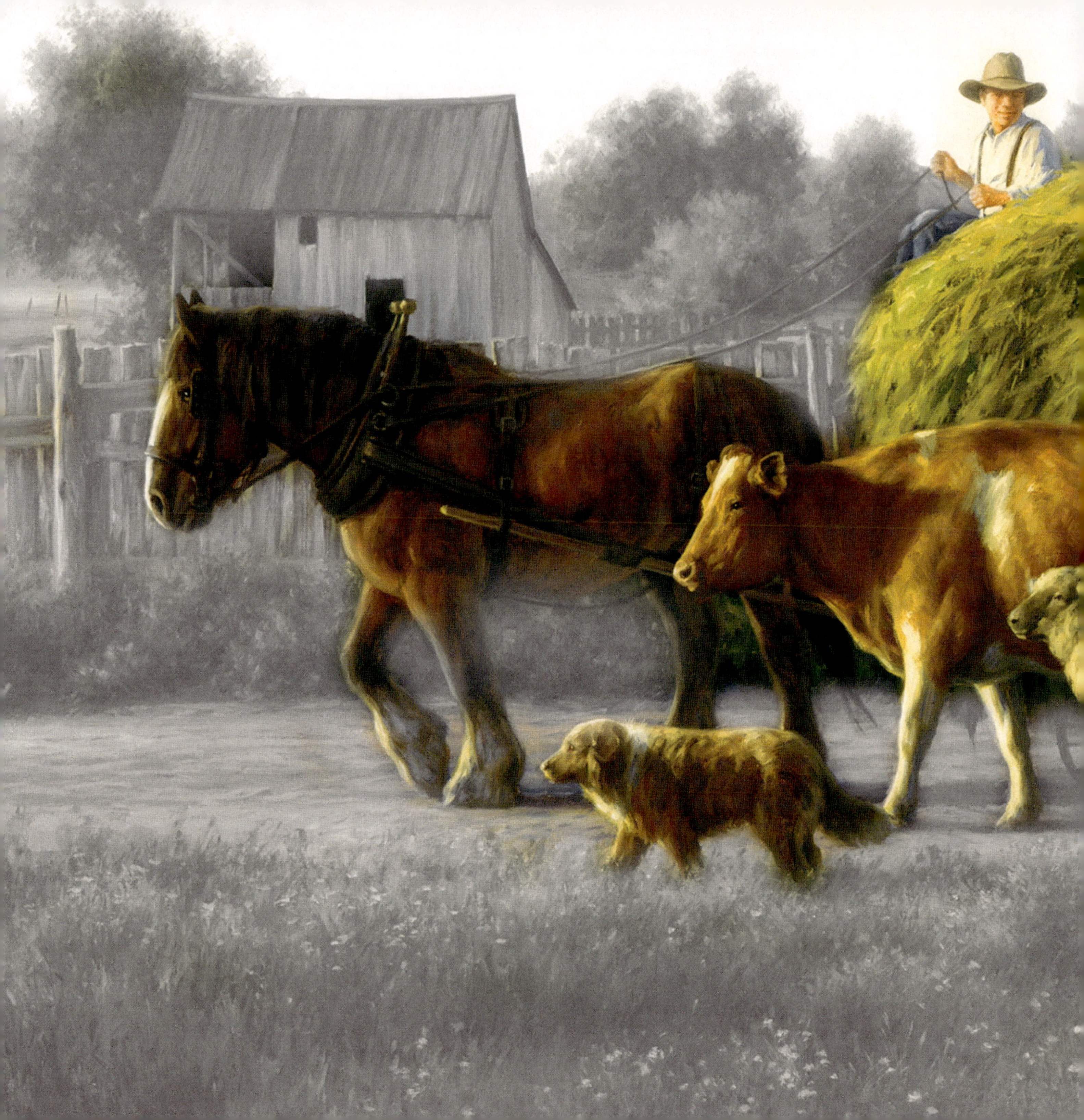

I could tell Daddy Clarence was enjoying the relaxing as much as I was. For the first time, with his eyes closed, his hat in his hand, and his head lying back against the hay, he looked to be old.

We came to the corral and Jesse backed the wagon into the existing stack. Daddy Clarence grabbed the hayfork and plunged it deep into the hay on the wagon.

"Ronnie and I will unload this, Jesse. I'll bet you're about bushed."

"Thanks, Clarence." Jesse sat down on the ground and Watch curled up beside him. I noticed that Jesse's hand went instinctively to the head of the coal black animal. I also found what it meant to have Daddy Clarence and I unload the hay. After about four fork loads, he turned to me and said, "I'll let you handle this. I'll go and unhitch the team. The task looked impossible. Each forkful hardly made a dent in the stack on the wagon. I'd plunge the fork into the hay and lift it up and swing it over my head dropping the load on top of the stack. I worked for what seemed quite a while. Sweat was dripping off my face. I hadn't noticed Jesse and Daddy Clarence let the horses into the corral. He came back and smiled at me. He gathered that at the rate I was going I would be their age before I was finished.

Jesse stepped up on the wagon and took the fork from my hands. What followed was a storm of hay. In about the time it took me to jump off the wagon, it was cleared. Daddy Clarence laughed as Jesse finished. He was proud of the show he'd put on. "You're one workin' machine, Mr. Roberts." Jesse smiled the smile of a man who had just received his first compliment.

Old Watch was at my heels and sniffing through what was left of his nose. I looked at his eyes, and I could see kindness there. Daddy Clarence saw me eyeing him. "What looks like meanness only a hour ago, Ronnie, was just

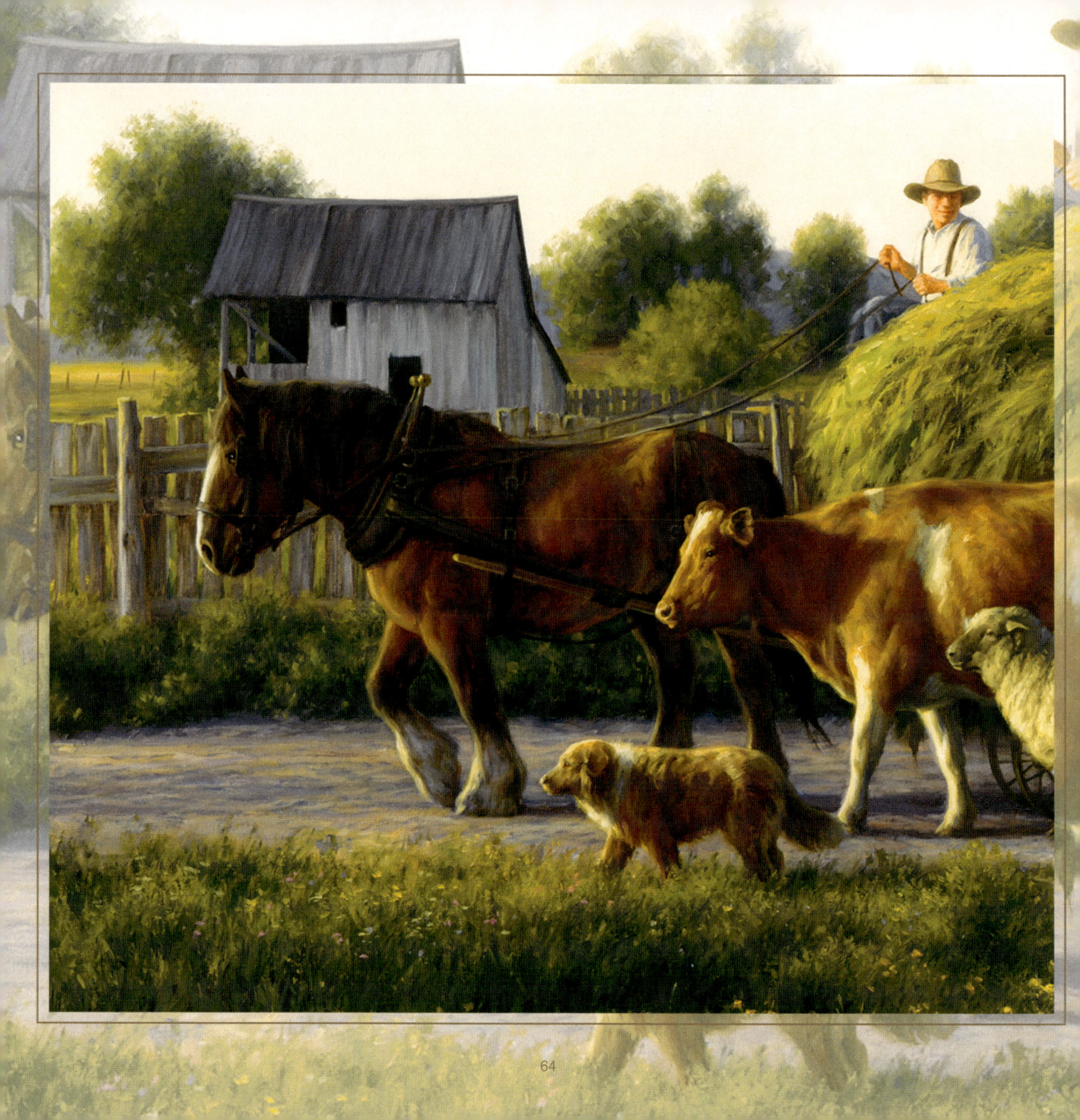

another manifestation of kindness for him. He was protectin' the home of his protector. That was all. Animals are pretty straight thinkers. It's usually us humans that get all tangled up and often think an animal is mean when he's really bein' kind in his own way."

Jesse said very few words that night. Daddy Clarence and I planned to sleep outside on our bedrolls with our horses hobbled. We could have put them in the corral but that would have led to some fighting. Daddy Clarence said there was no good to be done trying to establish a pecking order for an overnight visit. That night, before we retired, Daddy Clarence unloaded the packhorse and filled up Jesse's nearly empty food box.

He said, "Thanks, Clarence", and meant it.

"Mama Violet insists on takin' care of you." Daddy Clarence smiled accepting the gratitude but not wanting the credit. We ate some jerky and some leftover sour dough biscuits. As soon as it was dark, Jesse lay down on his bed and fell asleep. Watch retreated to his place on the little knoll with the granary. Daddy Clarence and I went for a little walk.

"There are a lot of animals many people never see, because they don't look during the night."

We walked down to the stream. When we got to the wide portion, Daddy Clarence sat on the low bank. He said we should be watching for deer that would be coming for something to drink. Sure enough, it wasn't three or four minutes before two doe came ambling down. They were some thirty feet away when they saw us. They stood frozen for a long moment. Then one of them started to swish her tail. When we didn't move, they both stepped closer to the water and began drinking.

"Animals can sense danger. And these don't feel any." After they had their fill of water, they scampered into the darkness.

The faded light of the sky made the trees look like silhouettes of lace. One by one the stars seemed to pop into view. The crickets were starting their song. A few nighthawks were diving through the air. It was night, a time when there seemed to be a spell come over everything.

"What are all those stars?" It was a question that seemed to ask itself.

"I don't reckon I know, Ronnie. But it's pretty hard to look up and not do a whole lot of wondering."

"About God and things?"

"You bet. I always felt this here kind of night created an awfully nice cathedral, even for us heathens."

"Are you a 'heathen', Daddy Clarence?"

"Don't reckon I am. But in the eyes of folks like the Reverend Charley Shiner, I probably qualify. There always seemed to me to be a difference between religion and believin'. But I've been wrong before and the right Reverend would probably say I am again. As far as I'm concerned, we're looking at some pretty convincing evidence of God's hand. I know some of the Good Book, and I've come to appreciate His writings in nature. But I don't believe there is any value in a religion that isn't actually true. And to have a god around just to explain things you can't explain don't make any sense to me either."

"How do you know there's a God, when nobody we know has ever seen Him?"

"I've done a lot of wonderin' about that very thing. I read the Bible. I believe it. In fact, I sometimes wonder if I don't believe it more that many of the church-goin' folks."

"Why don't you go to church?"

"Well, it has to do a lot with my wonderin'. Never could figure out the god those church-goers believed in. I was never a whiz but their creeds and my math just never did add up. In my mind, the Bible speaks pretty clearly about God bein' our Father and we bein' His children. I gather that He cared for us before we was ever formed in the belly. And by whatever means bodies were formed here, I suspect that what gives them life…and has them knowin' they're alive…is beyond this earth."

"You believe in Jesus?"

"Oh ya. But again, I see Him different than other folks do. I believe that the Bible has Him shepherdin' things on this world long before He was born in Bethlehem. He was involved in creatin' us and all this. I was interested to learn that many of the Foundin' Fathers of this country struggled with those old religious creeds. I'm no Christian of the creeds, but I am a Christian of the Bible."

He looked at me and guessed I wasn't understanding everything. But something inside of him made him keep going. "I believe there was a time when all people had the same faith. They worshipped the same God. But after a time they turned away and only God could set things right. This seems to be a pattern that repeats itself ever' few pages in the Bible. Then God sent His Son. It is incredible that they crucified Jesus. That final straw brought an age of darkness that lasted for centuries. It's my contentious belief that Christ was the center of that original gospel that God kept tryin' to get us to understand. We are here to learn to love…love those of our family…love all those of God's family."

"You sound like you're in church."

"Well, we are…we're in my church. Ronnie, years ago I was struck by what was bein' taught in Sunday School was the same things I was hearin' around the campfire with the Indians. The same creation story…the same flood story…the amazin' birth of a divine child… a savior. That all made me do some powerful wonderin' about why the Cherokee, the Apache, and other ancient peoples all have many of the same beliefs."

"Do you still wonder?"

"Ya, 'bout lots of things." With that Daddy Clarence fell silent and simply looked into the heavens. After a while he spoke. His voice was quiet.

"Boy, your great-great aunt on my Mother's side had a son who claimed to have helped bring to light an ancient writin' that explains why many Indian tribes have a legend about a White God appearin' to them. I read it for the first time many years ago. It had a big part in my believin' the Bible and formulatin' an idea of who God is…who I am…who we all are. I believe that ancient writin' is part of God settin' things right one last time. When you get older, I'll let you read it. You gotta decide these things for yourself. That was the way it was meant to be."

The night settled in nice and comfortable. Before long we laid the bedrolls out and climbed in. As we were dropping off to sleep, a couple of shooting stars moved halfway across the sky in opposite directions. Daddy Clarence looked over at me and smiled. "Looks like we ain't the only thing goin' on in the universe, Ronnie." I gathered he was right.

Before morning's light, I heard Jesse throwing hay to his horses. Watch made a pass at my bedroll and sniffed with his makeshift nose. We got up and went into the cabin. It was about twice as big as the bedroom with the pinecone wallpaper that I slept in. A wood stove dominated one end and a wooden food box the other. There was a table with one chair and a bed with a Levi quilt to balance out the room.

Jesse was well on his way to breakfast when we entered. The room smelled of cedar wood and the crackling of the stove gave indication of a hot fire. Jesse stood over the stove with a frying pan in which some bacon was sizzling. Once the bacon was cooked on both sides, he left it and went to the food box. He opened it and warm aromas escaped. He cut a slice of bread from the loaf we had brought. He smiled acknowledging the gift. Then he laid the slice of bread on the bacon in the pan. Once the bread was warm, he turned it over and let the bacon grease soak into it. He then picked up the frying pan and set it on the table. He put some salt and pepper on the bread and dug in with some obvious delight.

I stood and watched. I was fascinated by the uniqueness and simplicity of the meal. He ate directly from the pan using just the knife he had employed to cut the bacon and the bread. I looked at Daddy Clarence. He seemed busy looking at the plate and cup on the shelf by the bed.

Jesse didn't seem to mind that I was so interested in his eating regimen. With one hand under my chin and the other on the table, I soon discovered that I could make marks in the grime that had accumulated on the table over the years. After I had written my name in the layers of grease, Jesse looked at me and grinned through his less than tooth-full mouth. Within a few minutes, Jesse scraped the remainder of the food from the frying pan onto the floor. Watch devoured it in three gulps.

Jesse, turned to Daddy Clarence, "Thanks for comin'. Tell the missus." He left to hitch up his team and return to the fields.

"Well, Ronnie, I guess you and I best take advantage of this fire and cook our own breakfast."

"Jesse's breakfast was an interesting one."

"Yep. But it keeps him and that dog alive. Mama Violet gave him that plate and cup I was lookin' at over on the wall. It was Christmas and she'd seen how he ett. So she thought he would love a plate and cup. She wrapped it up all pretty. We rode up here on the day before Christmas and gave it to him. He loved it all right. I don't figure he'd ever had a Christmas present before. In fact he loved it so much, and it was so precious to him, that he's never used it.

"That's like a lot of folks. Sometimes the things they say they treasure the most…like family or nature or such…they revere them so highly…that they never devote any time to enjoying them."

Chapter 6

The days of summer came and blended into one another without anyone taking much notice. Part of most days was spent in the blacksmith shop, shoeing horses or sharpening plows or repairing something or other. However, most of what took place in the blacksmith shop was talk and idle boasting.

One day Lou Jesson brought his team of mules in to be shod. Daddy Clarence was busy fashioning some shoes from an old wagon spring when the conversation turned to running…foot speed. It was Jesson's claim that he was the fastest guy in the area. He had several little situations that seemed to back up his story. Daddy Clarence mostly listened between his pounding and hammering. Then I saw him wink at me.

"Lou, I believe I could beat you. I'm about twice your age, but I'll bet I can out distance ya between the shop and the road."

Now Lou was really taken back by this, seeing as there was such a spread in age. "Clarence, that don't make no sense. I could beat ya on my being younger all alone. That's hardly fair."

Daddy Clarence had sharpened his wagering methods enough to know that Lou needed just a bit more time before he bit. But it wasn't long before Lou and Daddy Clarence were in front of the shop and waiting for my hand to drop to start the run. Lou had put up his 30-30 rifle and Daddy Clarence had offered a year's worth of shoeing. After the race, all Lou could focus on was keeping the results quiet. Being beat by an old man was about all the shame a person could be expected to bear.

"Clarence, I don't believe it. How fast was you when you was young?"

"Lou, I've never seen anybody that could beat me. Fact is, I can out run most horses over a long enough trail."

This last comment must have landed in Lou's brain like an explosion. The only way to cover up the pain of a lost bet is to make a bigger one. And he jumped at the chance like a cougar on a cottontail.

"Clarence, you ain't sayin' you could beat one of my mules here to Mohlman's store are ya?"

"I'm sayin' I could beat one of your mules to Roosevelt."

Now that comment had even me reeling. Roosevelt was a good 30 miles away.

"Fact is, Lou, I'm supposed to go pick up a new horse there in the next day or so. You got somethin' you'd like to lose bettin' on whether you and your ol' Jack could beat me there?"

Now I had as a fact seen Daddy Clarence pick up Ol' Jane. I'd seen him out run Lou Jesson, but beating a mule to Roosevelt? Lou must have been following the same line of thinking, because he threw everything he could think of into the pot with a little boot, just to make certain the bet would be sealed. The race was on.

Daddy Clarence did make a stipulation. "Lou, I don't want you gettin' hurt on this thing publicly. So let's keep it just between us. You can imagine how embarrassing it will be for you, if you lose. If you win, you can do all the crowin' you like."

Lou agreed. Daddy Clarence announced to Mama Violet at dinner that he and I would take one horse to Roosevelt the next day to pick up the one that needed picking up. He didn't say anything about the race. I knew it wasn't my place to mention it.

The next morning we packed some food. I saddled Smokey. Daddy Clarence walked with me to Number Five where we met Lou Jesson. His mule was all slicked up. Lou had a smile on his face that would have made sitting royalty jealous.

"Clarence, you can still call this thing off, and I won't think any the worst of ya for it."

"Same goes for you, Lou. Jest look at what that mule has to carry and look at what I've got to carry. This thing is handicapped in my favor already."

For just a moment, I thought I saw a bit of wondering, if not doubt, cross Lou Jesson's face. But I must have been imagining it, for he turned his mule to the east and set out on a gallop.

Daddy Clarence looked up at me, "Are you up for this ride, Ronnie?"

I just laughed. "I can ride it if you can run it." And we were off.

Now Daddy Clarence had on a pair of moccasins to make his feet light. He started jogging. He never did tell Mama Violet what he was doing. I suspect he figured she'd have him committed for such foolishness.

Before sundown, we were in Roosevelt. I've never been so saddle sore in all my life. Daddy Clarence was so tired, for a couple of hours, I thought he was going to die. But we'd passed up Lou Jesson at Myton, about 7 miles out of Roosevelt. His mule was pretty stoved up. Daddy Clarence won the bet. He and I and Lou Jesson were the only ones that ever knew about it.

The next morning Daddy Clarence and I picked up the horse he'd traded for. He called her Rainbow the minute he saw her. She was a beauty under saddle. We took our time riding back to the ranch. In fact, we laid up in a place called Bluebell one night just to make sure the horses weren't being pushed too hard.

Now late the next day, just when we were crossing the canal before Number Five, I saw the highest degree of accomplishment in the trading art I've ever witnessed. We had taken our sweet time moseying along checking the wild flowers, prairie dogs and the like. It was nearly sundown. I could just see the tops of the tall pines that surrounded the ranch house. Daddy Clarence was in the middle of telling me about the streams that would be black with fish in the mountains come late August. He was just in the middle of that when he glanced behind us and saw the Reverend Charlie Shiner galloping toward us.

"Looks to me like the right Reverend is a man on a mission, Ronnie."

Daddy Clarence's eyes twinkled. "The Reverend always likes having the prettiest horse in the valley. I reckon I best test his ability to see into that glorious future he's always talkin' about."

I looked back. The rider in the black suit was closing ground rapidly. As he approached, I could see the look of earnestness that had been etched in his face from years of practicing. It was kind of a half smile that wasn't terribly friendly. The entire expression on his face was the look of anguished goodness.

"Clarence, mighty fine looking animal you're astride of there. Whereabouts did you find her?"

"Reverend, she's something of a miracle horse. Ya see, I was caught in Roosevelt this morning afoot. Had my grandson here. I was wondering how we were both gonna get back on one horse. And…well, you won't believe the story. But let me just say, bein' a Bible readin' man, you understand the significance of the rainbow. Well, I named her Rainbow. And you are right, she's a beauty!"

"Clarence, what would you take for her?"

I could see the eyes of the Reverend getting bigger with each word.

"Well, Brother Shiner, I cain't part with her. I just barely got her. I called her Rainbow because I could see she was full of promise. 'Sides, she's the prettiest thing under saddle these parts has ever seen."

Daddy Clarence kept his eyes forward so as not to tip his hand and just kept moving towards the ranch. It was like he was trolling for fish and the fish didn't care if there was a hook in the bait or not. The Reverend couldn't help himself.

"Clarence, I'll give you this horse of mine for her, right here on the spot."

"Reverend, I respect you as a man who knows a good piece of horseflesh when he sees one. But so am I."

We went but another hundred yards before the Reverend threw in his rifle and saddle.

"Reverend," Daddy Clarence's voice was low and sincere, "I ken see you've got a powerful hankerin'. And I ain't one to keep a man from something he wants so mightily."

Daddy Clarence stepped off Rainbow. The Reverend handed him the reins to his horse. Daddy Clarence loosened the cinch and pulled the saddle off Rainbow. As he did, a foot high pile of gunnysacks came off with it. The gunnysacks hit the ground about the same time as the Reverend's chin did. With his saddle in hand, Daddy Clarence swung on to the Reverend's horse and we started off. Daddy Clarence looked back at the still stunned Reverend and said, "Guess you can see why I call her Rainbow."

He was able to keep from laughing (but just barely) for about another hundred feet. Then he burst out in a roar so thunderous that I thought he might pass out. I must admit the sight of the Reverend standing there looking at that swayback horse with his mouth firmly in a slack jaw position was an astonishing moment.

Daddy Clarence, once he stopped laughing, swore me to silence…particularly to Mama Violet. He said that anything that interfered with her eternal church going enjoyment would not fare well for his earthly peace and happiness.

"And I'm quite certain, Ronnie, that the Reverend won't breath a word to anybody."

With that bit of counsel, his laughter resumed.

That evening after dinner, Daddy Clarence and I slipped out to the back porch. He sat on the old wooden kitchen chair that had been retired there for that very purpose. I sat down on the step. He pulled out his pocketknife and I followed suit. We each picked up a piece of kindling and began whittling. Now whittling is only whittling if it has no particular purpose in mind. Daddy Clarence said he had heard that great pieces of sculpture were already hiding in chunks of stone and were only discovered by artists as they began whittling away…as it were.

Over time it became quite obvious to us both that we were working with inferior material, because there wasn't anything of value hiding in the wood we had chosen to whittle. But that didn't take any of the enjoyment out of reducing respectable pieces of wood to mere toothpicks.

Of course, the other use of whittling is to give you something to do while you are gabbing. That way it doesn't feel like you are totally wasting time. That evening the conversation ran from story to story 'til Daddy Clarence finally began talking about the Indians.

He told me of the time that Marie Applinapp knocked on the door well after midnight with a hoe stuck in her head by an angry husband.

She had come to Mama Violet for help. He was about to continue when I asked what turned out to be a troubling question.

"Daddy Clarence, how come the Indians are dumber than we are?" With that the whittling stopped.

"Ronnie, whatever gave you that idea?"

"In my school, the teacher has all the students sitting at tables based on how smart they are. And all the Indian kids are on the dumb table."

"How do you feel about that?"

"I guess I hadn't thought too much about it 'til they started passing out new supplies in the middle of the year. They gave everyone new boxes of crayons, except they took the used boxes of crayons from the smart table and gave those to kids on the dumb table. They said it was to save money."

"How'd that make you feel?"

"Pretty bad, actually. The crayons in my box were all broken up. I was ashamed to have anyone trying to use them after me."

There was silence for several minutes. I could tell Daddy Clarence didn't take this conversation casually. "Ronnie, some of the brightest people I have ever knowed were Indians. But neither they nor I would account for much in any classroom. Our learning has always come about in the mountains with the streams, the clouds, and the animals. You sit me, or most Indians I know, in a hot room and tie us to a desk and tell us we are supposed to learn something someone else feels is important... well, I can tell you there ain't goin' to be much learnin' happen there. Because someone don't know something someone else knows doesn't make the first person dumb. Most teachers don't know a twig about blacksmithin'. They couldn't get a plow point out of a fire if..."

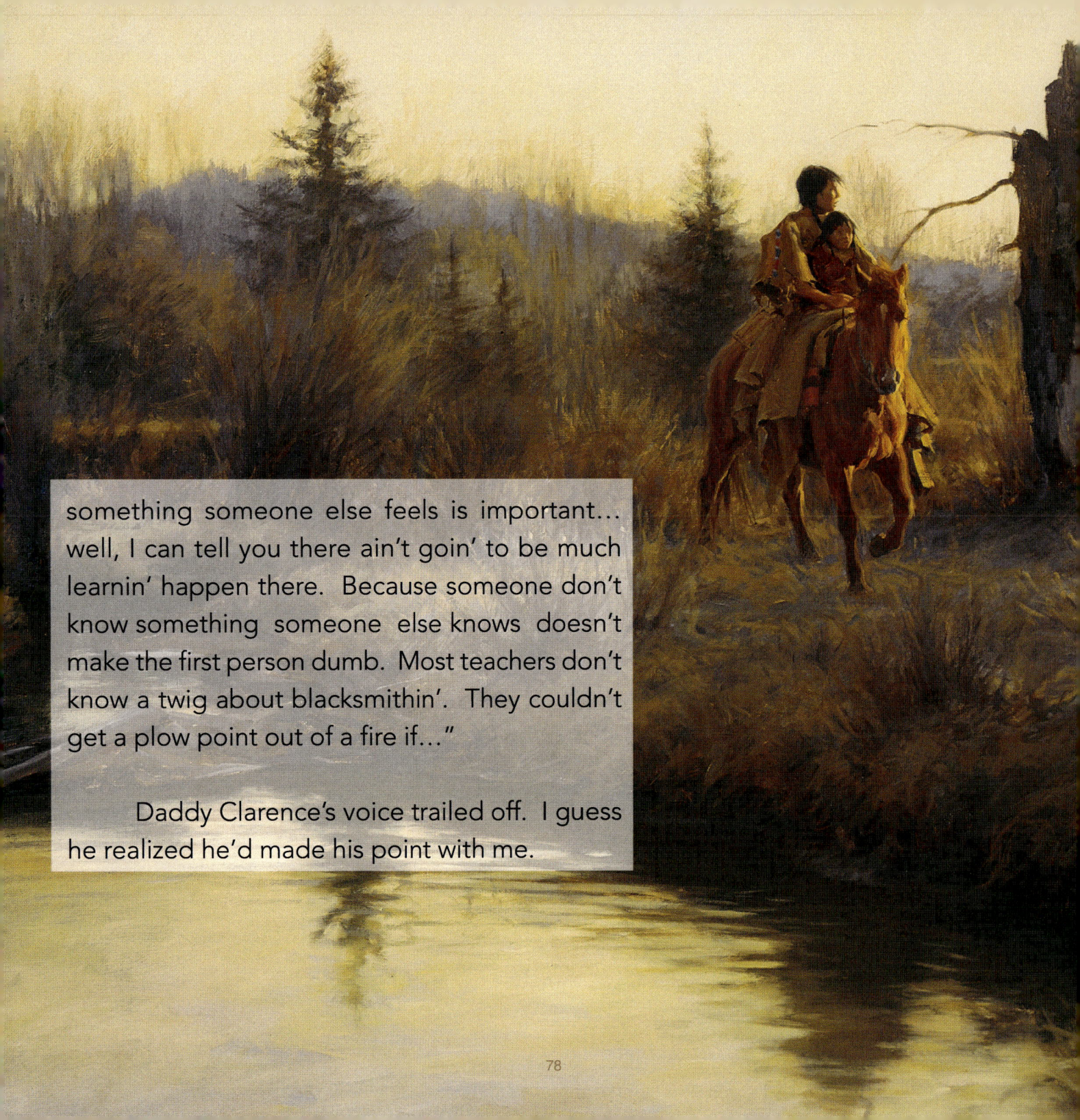

Daddy Clarence's voice trailed off. I guess he realized he'd made his point with me.

Chapter 7

The morning began with my waking to the smell of first coffee. I rolled out of bed anxious not to be left out of anything that life might hold. It was at that moment that I got my first objective look at what love is. I realized I loved Daddy Clarence. It was a feeling that didn't work itself into words very well. But I could see it as a distinct and marvelous entity all its own. Minutes, hours, days were simply better when I spent them with him. On this morning, I realized it was love that was pulling me willingly out of the warm covers. I walked into the kitchen just as he was sipping the last of the coffee from the saucer.

"Ronnie, right after milking this morning, I was thinking that we ought to move the cows down by the willows. I suspect that grass is getting pretty long. You feel up to doing a little walking?"

My smile was all the answer he needed. After the milking, he opened the corral gate and we headed the cows toward the south pasture by the willows. The cows obviously knew the way. So there was not a need for a lot of vigilance. Daddy Clarence began to tell me about the plants growing along the ditch bank.

"This here is wild iris." He pointed to a clump of large blossoms that were as intricate and pretty as I had heard orchids were supposed to be. We passed patches of wild daisies and of watercress. Then he pointed to a weed even I knew, foxtails.

"See that foxtail. I've seen that kill cows. Those little devils have little barbs on them. The cows eat them. They get lodged in their throats. They choke and die."

I have to admit, after he said that, I didn't hear much else of what he was saying. I could hardly believe that little weed I had seen all my life could actually kill a cow. I dropped a step or two behind Daddy Clarence. I stooped down and broke off one of the foxtails. I gently touched it to my tongue. I was amazed. It had little barbs on it. They would catch on my tongue with even the slightest touch. Then it caught! Before I knew it, the foxtail slipped into my throat.

I was going to die.

If foxtails could kill a cow, they could certainly kill a kid.

Tears streamed down my face. I began running not going anywhere in particular. I shot past Daddy Clarence. I heard him call my name, but I was dying. No other thoughts seemed to be able to make it into my mind. I ran past the herd of cows. I reached the clump of willows in the lower pasture before my lungs called a halt to my playing tag with fear. I dropped exhausted to my knees. Suddenly I felt the heavy breathing of Daddy Clarence on my back. He collapsed with his arm around me.

"What in tarnation got into you, boy?"

I couldn't answer. My stupidity at doing something I knew I shouldn't cast a spell of dumbness on me. Then I heard Daddy Clarence's voice reach a tone I had never heard before:

"TALK TO ME, NOW!"

"I'm dying," I blurted out. I grabbed my throat, "Foxtail."

With that revelation, Daddy Clarence collapsed beside me. "You swallowed a foxtail?"

I nodded my head, tears still streaming down my face.

"You wanted to see if foxtails really had barbs like I was saying? Your curiosity overwhelmed your good sense, did it?" He put his arm around me. "I rather suspect that running exhibition you just put on jiggled that foxtail all the way down to your toenails."

I looked up at his face. I could see tears in his eyes. But he was smiling. "You're not going to die. You're tougher than any cow."

Daddy Clarence's words gave life back to me. He held me. I cried for just a moment longer with the joy of living again. His large arms circled me into what seemed the safest place on earth.

"Some things are better believed than experienced." His words were spoken softly, but sounded awfully loud.

Chapter 8

Money was something that I never heard discussed. The reason, I suspect, was there wasn't any. If anyone needed anything or wanted anything, it had to be made, built, raised or grown. Buying something was simply not an option most of the time. What little money there was, Mama Violet kept in the old sugar bowl in the cupboard. It was residue from the monthly creamery check.

Now this would be of little note, except on the 4th of July, Mama Violet got up with Daddy Clarence and surprised him with a new pistol she had ordered from the Sears and Roebuck catalogue way back in the spring. She presented it to him saying she had saved the money out of the creamery money. Daddy Clarence was as tickled as a kid.

"I have never owned a new gun my entire life. Ever'thing I had was used or traded for." He held Mama Violet in his arms for a long time. You'd have thought they had just got married all over again. Mama Violet was even happier than Daddy Clarence. She knew how pleased the new gun would make him. She always seemed to get very happy when Daddy Clarence was happy.

"Ronnie, right after milkin', you and I are gonna have to try this thing out."

Milkin' seemed to go awfully fast. Daddy Clarence let me hold the gun a good share of the time. Of course, it wasn't loaded or anything. It was heavy and felt awfully strong. We walked through the north forty after the chores.

"Ronnie, there's a bit of power that a man feels when he's carrying a gun. It's something you need to be careful with. 'Cause the mere presence of the gun makes a person feel more powerful than he should have a mind to."

"You ever see a gun fight?"

Daddy Clarence stared at me for a moment. "Don't reckon I've actually seen one. But I arrived on the scene of one shortly after it happened. I was in California at the time and got word that my Mother needed me. So I was hightailing it back home and crossed through Goldfield, Nevada. Just as I got there, they were cleaning up after two guys. They had gone at it following an argument over a card game."

We were walking through the pasture looking for things that we might legitimately try the gun on. Sun was clearing the mountains to the east. Nothing seemed to be moving except for a little mother killdeer. This little bird was squawking up a storm. She would run along the ground doing her broken-wing act. Nature had taught her to use this act to lead people and prey away from her nest. The theory being that if she looked easy to catch, we would follow her rather than look for her young. While we weren't following her, our direction of travel must have appeared to her like a successful attempt to get us away from her nest. Daddy Clarence didn't seem to pay her any mind, but her noise began to irritate me just a bit. Then Daddy Clarence got my mind off her with his gun talk.

"My Father taught me to never shoot

at anything I didn't need to eat. Found that to be a pretty good rule." He chuckled for a moment to himself, obviously relishing a personal piece of information. "Ronnie, let me tell you somethin' I've never told anybody. I've gone deer hunting every year of my life. And I've never been able to bring myself to shoot a deer. Now for some fool reason, I've never been able to admit that to anyone."

I looked up at him and I could see he was talking to himself as much as to me.

"Most folks in this area know I ken out shoot just about anybody. But they all take comfort in knowin' that they can bring home a deer and I can't. Funny thing, too, I take all kinds of venison in trade for work. So it isn't I can't eat 'em. They're just too pretty or something."

Daddy Clarence then realized that he had just verbalized something to himself with me in hearing distance. "Ronnie, don't you go tellin' nobody about that." I nodded, though I didn't quite realize what the great secret was all about.

We reached the top of the north forty. Daddy Clarence stopped and loaded some shells into the new pistol. There was a row of weeds we referred to as Indian tobacco along the stream. Without saying anything, Daddy Clarence broke six of them off at the stem just below the seeds.

"Seems to shoot pretty true," he said casually.

"Would you like to try it?"

Would I!

Now I had never shot a gun before unless you count a BB gun…which doesn't count. Daddy Clarence loaded in a shell and handed me the gun. Standing beside me, he showed me how to hold it with both hands and sight it. I spread my feet apart and raised both hands that were firmly holding the pistol. I looked down the sight and there, about a hundred yards away, was the mother killdeer. She was so far away I could barely see her, but I could still hear her infernal squawking. So I thought, "I'll just scare her." I got her in the sights and raised the pistol just a hair. I pulled the trigger.

She fell..silent.

I gasped a couple of breaths. I looked at Daddy Clarence. I could tell his reaction was suspended somewhere between:

1. Nice shot!

And…

2. How do you feel about killing a mother bird who was just trying to protect her young…and whose little ones will now suffer a slow, painful death.

He could see clearly by the tears volunteering their way into my eyes and down my cheeks, I was consumed by the latter reaction. All I could say was, "I didn't mean to do it. I didn't mean to do it!"

Daddy Clarence put his arm around me. I handed him the new pistol that didn't look all that exciting anymore. We walked in silence. As we approached the ranch house, Daddy Clarence's voice filled the emptiness. "You just learned a great lesson today my boy. When you get as old as I am, you will have had the experience of hearin' a lot of people cry, 'I didn't mean to do it. I didn't mean to do it.' Yet, iffen you stopped and looked down the sights of their life, they ended up hittin' just exactly what they was aimin' at."

"But I killed a mother bird. Her young will suffer."

"Yes. And you'll hurt some from that for a time. But it's best that you learn young the lesson that you'd better be careful what you are aiming at. 'Cause it isn't beyond reason to think you'll hit it. A lot of folks think they can dance with the Devil and then simply walk on after the music stops. But that ain't the case. Once you start on a particular path, you better make certain you know where it ends up, because one day you'll find yourself there."

It sounded like one of those lessons that was important. But I would have to live some before I grasped its true significance. I could feel his powerful hand pull me towards him. I seemed to melt into his being.

In a similar way…the days, the weeks, and I suspect, the months…melted together. The dream of going to the mountain remained a dream. The next thing I knew Dad was home and school was starting the next week.

The summer had passed.

Epilogue

Many summers have passed. School, college, career have all come and gone. I now have grandchildren of my own. Daddy Clarence died at age ninety-three. Before passing, he lapsed into a coma. I rushed to the hospital. As I walked into the room, he awoke. He spoke to me, much to the astonishment of the attending nurse.

As we concluded our conversation, he said, "You'll come back soon, won't you, Ron." I nodded. I've kept that promise. Often, very often, I go back in my mind to that magical time and place that was its own kind of heaven…summer…in Altonah…with Daddy Clarence. And at some future day, we'll take that trip to the mountains…together.

Made in the USA
Columbia, SC
20 September 2019